Library of
Davidson College

Library of
Davidson College

U.S. EXPORT CONTROL POLICY

U.S. Export Control Policy

Executive Autonomy vs. Congressional Reform

WILLIAM J. LONG

COLUMBIA
UNIVERSITY
PRESS
New York

Columbia University Press
New York   Guildford, Surrey
Copyright © 1989 Columbia University Press
All rights reserved

LIBRARY OF CONGRESS
Library of Congress Cataloging-in-Publication Data

Long, William J., 1956–
U.S. export control policy:
executive autonomy vs. congressional reform / William J. Long.
p.   cm.
Bibliography: p.
Includes index.
ISBN 0-231-06798-4 (alk. paper)
1. Export controls—United States.
2. United States—Commercial Policy.
I. Title.   II. Title: US export control policy.
HF1455.L63 1989
382'.64'0973—dc19   88-22064
CIP

Book Design by Charles Hames

Printed in the United States of America

Casebound editions of Columbia University Press books are
Smyth-sewn and printed on permanent and durable acid-free paper

CONTENTS

PREFACE vii

1. A Theory of U.S. Export Control Policy 1
2. The Origins of the
   U.S. Export Control System, 1949–1969 13
3. Export Control Law and Policy in the 1970s 29
4. Institutional Influence on Licensing:
   The Reforms of 1974, 1977, and 1979 55
5. Executive Autonomy and
   Foreign Policy Export Controls 69
6. Recent Developments in Export Policy 91
7. Patterns of Executive Authority 101

NOTES 109

BIBLIOGRAPHY 157

INDEX 169

PREFACE

As a graduate student, I was reminded by Professor William T. R. Fox that, in social science research, it is permissible to paint the bull's-eye after you have shot the arrow, i.e., to decide where your research is going after you have gotten there. My study of U.S. export control policy ends not too differently from its original intent, however.

I have had the opportunity to study U.S. export policy both as a scholar and as a practitioner of U.S. trade law at private firms. As a practitioner, I often heard U.S. exporters rail against the alleged complexity or slowness of the system and their inability to anticipate its workings. As a researcher considering the history of U.S. export policy, I was impressed by the similarity between contemporary expressions of dissatisfaction over the operation of the U.S. export control system and similar complaints raised by exporters throughout the 1960s and 1970s.

I subsequently discovered that Congress, in response to these concerns, periodically attempted in various ways to address and redress them only to conclude several years later that its efforts had been largely unsuccessful and that they must try again to reform the system. I also discovered that the executive branch often opposed congressional reforms, articulated distinct interests during the legislative process, and often successfully prevailed upon Congress to limit or alter reform legislation as a result. Furthermore, in studying the implementation of export control laws, I learned that in myriad ways the President and the relevant executive agencies carried out policy in keeping less with Congress's intent and more with its own.

It therefore struck me that, as an important aspect of U.S. trade policy, prevailing pluralist notions of societal, that is, business interests, effectively influencing policy through Congress was an inadequate if not inappropriate explanation of U.S. export control policy. Furthermore, as part of U.S. foreign policy generally, the maintenance of executive department influence in (if not dominance of) U.S. export control policy in the 1970s and 1980s seemed problematic in light of the resurgence of congressional authority in foreign policy in the late 1970s and the vastly increased economic importance of exports to the U.S. economy during that period.

Clearly a better understanding of the role of the executive and executive institutions was required to understand U.S. export control policy. That, in essence, is what this study set out to do and, I believe, has accomplished. Along the way, I offer an explanation as to the sources of executive authority, the content of its policies, and the procedures by which it carries out its policies and maintains its authority.

Having completed this book, I realize how much I owe to so many. Of particular importance to the development and execution of the study was the insight and guidance I received from Professor Robert Jervis of Columbia University, who supervised earlier drafts. In this regard, I am also indebted to Professor David Baldwin also of Columbia University for his valuable comments and criticisms.

I have also benefited greatly from several scholars and practitioners who gave generously of their time and expertise in helping me focus my effort and understand the complexities of U.S. export control policy, including; Professor Gary Bertsch of the University of Georgia; Professor I. M. Destler of the University of Maryland; Professor Henry Nau of George Washington University; Mr. William Root, former Director of the Office of East-West Trade at the U.S. Department of State; Mr. Maurice Mountain, formerly of the U.S. Department of Defense; Mr. Roger Mayjak of Textronics, Inc.; Mr. Arthur Downey of Sutherland, Asbill & Brennan; Mr. Stanley Marcuss of Milbank, Tweed, Hadley & McCloy; and Dr. Thomas Blaisdell, former Assistant Secretary of Commerce. Any inaccuracies or mistakes in this study, however, are my responsibility. In the production of the manuscript, I am most grateful for the patient and careful work of Ms. Wanda Cross and Ms. Brenda Cruz.

Finally, and most indispensable, is the help and encouragement I have received from family and friends. In this regard, there are too many to thank individually, but I owe a special debt of gratitude to my parents, and mostly to my wife, Mary.

U.S. EXPORT CONTROL POLICY

1. A THEORY OF U.S. EXPORT CONTROL POLICY

WHEN the United States emerged as an economic and political superpower after World War II, it attempted to create a liberal international economic regime while simultaneously protecting its strategic interests; this led to the development of an extensive, peacetime export control system. The United States did not emerge from the war anxious to assume its international responsibilities—most of the domestic population did not appreciate these obligations. American internationalism first surfaced before the war in the form of the Reciprocal Trade Agreements Act, and the initial postwar institutional response was multilateral: that period saw the creation of the International Monetary Fund, the International Bank for Reconstruction and Development, the United Nations agencies, and a projected International Trade Organization. American policymakers quickly realized, however, that such a postwar system could not be initiated without American leadership in the context of a declining British Empire, a nonexistent Chinese government, a phantom French power, and a little-understood Soviet Union. As the fundamental source of plentiful food and fuel and functioning industry, the U.S. government made use of its war-initiated mechanisms to reestablish a peacetime economy—both domestically and internationally. Lend-lease gave way to a peacetime Marshall Plan, and wartime trade controls developed into a permanent peacetime export control apparatus which is the focus of this book.

America's peacetime export control apparatus relies primarily on export sanctions and export licensing. Sanctions have been used in exceptional situations to pressure other countries to alter their policies vis-à-vis the United States or third parties and for symbolic or signaling purposes.

Licensing has limited the shipment of specific goods and technologies to countries with military and foreign policy interests adverse to those of the United States. Although directed at prohibiting the transfer of selective goods and technology to particular destinations, export controls are nonetheless broad in scope: the system is, in theory, inclusive. All goods and technology exported are either generally licensed, i.e., exportable without explicit permission to export, or require formal application for an individual or multiple export license. Seldom recognized is the fact that the export licensing system requires formal license approval for upwards of 50 percent of all U.S. manufacturers exports (valued at $62 billion in 1985).[1] Also, because the system is concerned not only with the direct transfer of proscribed items to U.S. adversaries but with the diversion of goods and technology to them through America's allies and neutrals, the system falls heavily on U.S. trade with allied and neutral countries. For example, approximately 90 percent of export licenses govern the export or reexport of goods or technology from one Western nation to another.[2]

Discussions of U.S. policy on export controls have focused primarily on their exceptional use as instruments of economic coercion.[3] Their origin, codification, institutionalization, and operation as part of America's postwar foreign economic policy have received little attention and have generated insufficient explanation.

This book will explore the making and implementation of U.S. export control laws in the postwar period. Underlying this investigation is the central proposition that the executive and the relevant bureaucratic agencies (particularly the Departments of Commerce, Defense, and State) helped to shape export control law and policy and were more autonomous political actors vis-à-vis Congress and domestic interest groups than is appreciated under prevailing pluralist notions of the role of the American executive and executive agencies in U.S. export control and trade policy.[4] Moreover, executive dominance has persisted beyond the immediate Cold War period when, arguably, the perception of a national security crisis and the relative unimportance of international trade to the American economy might have promoted congressional and interest group deference to the executive. Since 1969—although the perceived threat to national security has receded, Congress is more assertive in foreign policy, and the business community's interest in export markets has vastly increased—the executive *still* dominates export control policy. Furthermore, in recent years the executive has extended the original East-West national security thrust of the policy to encompass export controls directed at non–East bloc countries to serve a variety of foreign policy objectives, including human rights, antiterrorism, and nuclear nonproliferation.

This book will examine U.S. export controls historically to discern a pattern of executive branch dominance, to assess the instrumentalities of the executive in defining and implementing policy, and to provide some insight into the content and impact of, and the motivations for, the executive's activities.

■ Theories of the Role of the Executive, Congress, and Interest Groups

Simply stated, there is no well-developed theory on the role of domestic actors in U.S. export control policy. Nonetheless, pluralism has been offered as a theoretical explanation.[5] Furthermore, although export control policy is seldom considered directly, many writers on U.S. import policy imply that pluralism explains U.S. export policies as well.

This book suggests that pluralism offers an insufficient explanation of U.S. export control policy. Pluralism views the political process as dominated by interest group activities. It suggests that the representative and leadership functions of democracy are the result of bargaining and competition among numerous randomly arranged interest groups: thus it tends to ignore the systematic effects of central state actors.[6]

For example, Gary Bertsch argues that, despite the high degree of centralization of authority within the executive, the politics of East-West trade and technology transfer (roughly synonymous with the politics of export controls) are best understood through an appreciation of the "structural pluralism" of the American political system.[7] Bertsch aptly summarizes why he believes pluralism should account for U.S. export control policy, especially in the past two decades:

> There are a number of reasons for this development ... includ[ing] the weakening of presidential power in the post-Vietnam and Watergate eras; the increasing assertiveness of a Congress disposed to recapture its constitutional role in American foreign policy; ... the increasing importance and power of U.S. commercial, and particularly agricultural, interests in

a period of declining export performance, and U.S. reactions to Soviet foreign policy intrigues...."[8]

Bertsch concludes that as a consequence of these forces, the Cold War consensus on East-West trade and technology transfer has declined as the political process has become increasingly pluralistic, "marked by more political actors and centers of power with access to the making and implementation of U.S. foreign economic policy."[9]

Theoretical approaches to overall U.S. trade policy are consistent with the pluralist emphasis on particular interests focused on Congress.[10] Many studies of U.S. import policy imply that their pluralistic explanations apply with equal force to U.S. export policy. Consequently, many analyses of the role of the executive in U.S. trade policy ignore or underestimate the executive's importance, its strength, and its insularity from domestic interests.

Most notable in this regard are works by Benjamin J. Cohen and Robert Pastor. Cohen defines "foreign commercial policy" as representing "the sum total of actions by the state intended to affect the extent, composition, and direction of its imports *and exports* of goods and services" (emphasis added).[11] Yet Cohen looks to Congress and domestic interests to explain foreign commercial policy. While Cohen notes that a nation's *general* foreign policy "is not only a function of specific lesser interests within the nation ... [but] must ultimately be legitimized by the state's national interest, and its national interest, however specifically defined, encompasses a set of general purposes that transcend the particular ambitions of domestic institutions," he fails to recognize the applicability of his general postulate to U.S. foreign trade policy—most particularly, to export control policy. On the contrary, Cohen asserts that in the area of foreign commerce, the state's interventions into the international system can be explained either on economic grounds (wealth maximization) or as "plainly the product of special interest legislation, the outcome of the effect of powerful domestic institutions achiev[ing] their own particular goals at the expense of the national community as well as the outside world."[12]

Similarly, Robert Pastor views trade policy as including "those state actions that affect trade unintentionally as well as those intended to affect it. Moreover, trade is a tool for development, and therefore a key element in the north-south dialogue, *and a strategic weapon, and therefore an important item in East-West relations*" (emphasis added).[13] Nonetheless, Pastor suggests that "trade policy is the product of interaction of the two branches" wherein both branches continually prod each other.[14] He focuses on import policy and the problem of free trade versus protectionism. While noting that Congress delegated some trade negotiating authority to the executive through the Reciprocal Trade Agreements Act of 1934 and thereby relinquished sole authority over trade policy, Pastor adds that the President has not come to dominate either trade policy or processes since that time.[15] Rather, according to Pastor, import policy became an international as well as a domestic matter after 1934, and the general rules for trade negotiations were and still are made through cooperation between Congress and the executive.[16]

Theories on general U.S. foreign policy, while accounting for executive dominance in export control policy during the early Cold War period, do not adequately explain the *continuation* of executive dominance in this area in the post-1969 period. Scholars have described the President as the primary force in foreign affairs during the second half of the twentieth century. Furthermore, the President's ascent to prominence in foreign affairs was thought to relegate Congress to a secondary role.[17] Congress's influence in foreign policy was viewed primarily as legitimating and amending policies initiated by the executive. In Robert Dahl's often-cited words, it is "an exaggeration perhaps, but one not too wide of the mark, to say that in foreign policy the President proposes, the Congress disposes—and in a very large number of highly important decisions about foreign policy, the Congress does not even have the opportunity to dispose."[18] Most analysts attribute the President's primacy to the "complex nature of public policies,"[19] the dispersion of power and responsibility within Congress, and the executive's "superior resources for handling the vast new amounts of information available to the total policy-making process."[20]

More recent discussions of U.S. foreign policy claim that the depiction of extensive executive dominance is more accurate with respect to the 1945–65 period than it is to subsequent decades. By the mid-1970s, Congress had reasserted itself in U.S. foreign policymaking; repealing the Gulf of Tonkin Resolution, overriding President Nixon's veto of the War Powers Act, terminating the President's authority to provide emergency military aid to South Vietnam, prohibiting continued CIA expenditures in support of anticommunist forces in Angola, and establishing a permanent intelligence oversight committee. In short, the anticommunist values that forged a bipartisan consensus on U.S. foreign policy in the 1950s and 1960s had eroded by the 1970s.

Thus, within the general foreign policy literature, this book seeks to explain why the executive continues to dominate export control policy despite the growing importance of exports to domestic business interests, a far less accommodating Congress in matters of foreign policy, and the passing of Cold War norms.

In addition to the influences of liberalism and pluralism, American constitutionalism has also contributed to an underestimation of the executive's role in trade policy. Legal scholarship too readily assumes that Congress is, necessarily, the most important actor in the regulation of foreign commerce.[21] Constitutional discussions of the relative power of the executive branch in economic policy suggest that regulation of international commerce is primarily the province of Congress, not the executive. Such a conclusion appears logical in view of the Constitution's limits on the President's foreign affairs power and the practical and historic strictures on the President emanating from the Constitution as interpreted by the executive and the courts.

Under the Constitution, the President is limited to commanding the army and navy, appointing ambassadors, and making treaties with the advice and consent of the Senate. The Constitution does not authorize the executive to conduct foreign trade policy. Rather, the Constitution gives Congress explicit authority to regulate commerce with foreign nations, declare war, and make all laws necessary and proper to carry out its appointed powers.[22] Under this grant of authority, Congress has historically wielded legislative authority over the entire field of foreign trade regulation, including the imposition of tariffs and nontariff barriers to imports. For example, before 1934, tariff policy was made unilaterally by Congress subject only to presidential persuasion and the possibility of a veto.[23] After passage of the Reciprocal Trade Agreements Act of 1934,[24] the President had a direct but limited and congressionally delegated role in trade policy. Historically, for political[25] more than constitutional reasons, trade agreements with foreign nations have been made by executive agreement. Executive agreements are based on the authority delegated by both houses of Congress and implemented by subsequent legislation, rather than by more exclusively executive means such as a sole executive agreement or a self-executing treaty.

This book will demonstrate that existing theories fail to capture fully the importance of the executive and its institutions and, consequently, fail to explain their motivations and methods in shaping U.S. export control policy during the past forty years. It maintains that the executive has operated as an important and relatively autonomous political actor in this area. The origins of the executive's abilities stemmed from instrumentalities fashioned to cope with wartime emergencies which continued in peacetime because of the international and domestic orientation of the United States.

Periodically since 1969, the executive, to a greater degree than Congress or interest groups, has successfully articulated and pursued export control policies that emphasize national security, foreign policy, and ideological goals (apart from wealth maximization through free trade), in opposition to the emphasis by the congressional majority and interest groups on export expansion. In addition to substantive differences, the executive has fought to maintain its procedural flexibility and its prerogative to use export controls as it sees fit; it has, over the years, developed a variety of policy instruments through which to exercise its authority. Once a degree of executive autonomy has been established, irrespective of the particular policy goal pursued, the executive has often supported policies which reinforce its authority, flexibility, and control over society.[26]

■ The Role of Bureaucratic Institutions

The second underlying theme of this book suggests that U.S. export control policy has also been shaped significantly by bureaucratic institutions. Institutions, it is argued, are "neither neutral reflections of exogenous environmental forces nor neutral arenas for the performances of individuals driven by exogenous preferences and expectations."[27] Emphasizing the executive's role further permits an assertion that policy outcomes are, in part, the result of institutional dynamics occurring within the executive.[28]

While this particular characterization of the role of institutions in shaping America's foreign economic policy has several antecedents,[29] it can be differentiated from traditional democratic, instrumental or, to a degree, bureaucratic politics explanations of the role of institutions in policymaking. A democratic politics theory maintains that the bureaucracy performs a representative function much like that of elected officials. Under this theory, the bureaucracy, as part of a coequal branch of government, directly represents the public which has delegated to it a limited amount of authority and discretion.

Similarly, a bureaucratic politics analysis applies pluralists' notions of democracy to internal executive branch policymaking. Government agencies supplant interest groups, and policy outcomes are viewed as the result of bargaining and coalition formation among competing bureaus, as opposed to competing private interest groups.[30] A major alternative approach stresses the instrumental or neutral substantive and administrative functions performed by the bureaucracy. This latter approach suggests that the bureaucracy's representative responsibility is to the interests of the state and society as a whole rather than to any one member, group, or coalition.[31]

In considering the role of bureaucratic institutions, this book hypothesizes that the bureaucracy plays an autonomous and substantive role in export control policymaking, rather than an instrumental or representational role. A corollary is the assertion that, because policy is implemented through an independent bureaucracy, Congress's enunciation or revision of a policy does not necessarily lead to a corresponding change in policy outcome. Unlike the clash of presidential and congressional interests that have provided focal points for assessing executive capacity, institutional affects on policy are gradual, continuous, and rarely overtly political. Nonetheless, export control institutions shape policy by pursuing self-defined, discernible mandates. As a result, institutional practices can produce results different from those designed by Congress or hoped for by domestic interests.

The necessary second step in explaining the bureaucracy's role involves defining *how* the bureaucracy shapes export control policy. A case study of implementation affords an opportunity to test several more specific hypotheses on institutional motivations and operations.

In this regard, this book suggests that the bureaucracy is motivated by a desire to fulfill established duties and symbolic goals more than a rational, instrumental pursuit of exogenously, i.e., congressionally chosen goals embodied in export control legislation or a representative pursuit of interest group demands. Despite societal changes, established career officials, because they are insulated from immediate societal pressures, possess a greater ability to implement established policies, resulting over time in relatively continuous policies. This book further hypothesizes that the origin of the bureaucracy's motivations lies in the ideological climate, the structure of the international system, and the alignment of domestic interests prevailing at its inception.[32] Specifically, U.S. export control institutions derived, and in large measure continue to derive, their mandate from laws which were born and operated for two decades in a period of Cold War political rivalry, unparalleled American international economic hegemony, and domestic political consensus on export controls. In short, institutional histories as well as institutions are an important determinant of policy outcomes.

Because of the complexity of export control, inter- and intra-institutional processes, and the varying effects of institutional dynamics on export control policy, no single theory of institutional operation will be offered here.[33] As examples of bureaucratic influence over policy, this book will set forth data on institutional practices that reflect rigidities and the pursuit of indigenous institutional goals. Moreover, it is suggested here that the technical complexity of export controls creates a policy area particularly susceptible to the exercise of institutional authority.

Because export control policymaking is complex and diffused among several agencies, the system's operation at times reflects varying priorities among competing bureaus. As could be predicted by a bureaucratic politics approach, operations often end in stalemate, delay, and inconsistent policy.[34] But too much should not be made of a bureaucratic politics explanation.[35] Although the executive branch is divided on some issues some of the time, it is not a system "rent by organizational fissures."[36] While divisions exist and organizational mandates are often self-defined, the bureaucracy is not necessarily aligned—as one might expect—with the interests of particular societal groups, and bureaucratic stands are not necessarily determined by where a particular bureaucracy sits. For example, the Commerce Department's Office of Export Administration, the most important bureaucracy in export control operations and supposedly the one attentive to business interests, consistently adopts practices at odds with business interests and defines its mandate as serving primarily the nation's security interests. Because the source for the Commerce Department's mandate in export control policy is, in part, the aforementioned combination of domestic, international, and ideological forces which prevailed during the 1945–65 period, a bureaucratic politics model that presumes the Commerce Department's mandate is export expansion while the Defense Department's is national security would fail to recognize that both Commerce and Defense have pursued export control policies that emphasize the goal of national security to a greater degree than Congress or domestic interest groups—although the Defense Department has been more zealous than Commerce in this pursuit.

Moreover, although a bureaucratic politics approach suggests that the President is often unable to articulate or implement policy because of the inertia and self-serving procedures of permanent government, the President has in fact demonstrated a great deal of authority and efficacy in articulating policy through the heads of the relevant bureaucracies and, when motivated, has moved with great alacrity in marshaling its powers to serve, via "foreign policy" export controls, particular ideological interests. In short, while the bureaucratic politics model rightly draws attention to the role of the bureaucracy in policymaking, it does not offer a complete or completely accurate description of export control policy implementation or the role of the bureaucracy.

■ Method and Organization

This book approaches its topic chronologically, beginning with a discussion of the inception and development of the statutory and institutional framework. Specifically, it will consider the history of the most important piece of domestic legislation that empowers the executive to control exports and implement export sanctions in peacetime—the Export Control Act, later the Export Administration Act[37]—and its bureaucracy.[38] After a discussion of the origins of America's export control regime, the book will consider how subsequent laws and policies were shaped by the executive and executive institutions; how the executive, after establishing a role in export control policy, became a relatively autonomous actor and influenced policy outcome.

Treating the executive as a more autonomous actor requires a demonstration of two things: (1) that the executive, although influenced by its domestic and international environment, defines and pursues interests distinct in some measure from any particular interest or collection of interests; and (2) that the executive has, to some extent, demonstrated an ability to accomplish its aims.[39] This book will compare and contrast the positions adopted by the executive and executive institutions and those assumed by the congressional majority and domestic interest groups during the passage of export control legislation. It will then consider outcomes in the issue areas that were central points of contention during the lawmaking process and assess and explain the executive's ability or inability to prevail in the areas where it has articulated an interest at odds with the congressional majority and domestic interest groups.

In the area of export control, Congress channels and articulates particular domestic interests while the executive formulates its own statement of the national interest. The executive institutions involved are the President and the Departments of Commerce, Defense, and State. Testimony before Congress during the passage and amendment of export control laws reveals the interests of the executive, the private exporting community, and Congress. Publicly available position papers and interviews with actors in the private sector, on Capitol Hill, and in executive agencies have augmented this investigation of policymaking.

Under statutory arrangements, Congress left policy *implementation* almost exclusively to the executive. To a degree, the executive's use of its authority and its motivations for and fashioning of policy are a matter of public record. For example, public notice must be given for most presidential and many bureaucratic exercises of export control authority. The executive must report to Congress regarding many export control policies, and executive findings accompanying the exercise of export control authority must often be promulgated. Similarly, bureaucratic practices that are embodied in the regulations implementing statutes are, in part, matters of public record,[40] and internal, subregulatory practices have, on several occasions, been subject to publicly available government and private audits. Through an examination of the publicly available material and interviews with governmental officials, including both appointed and permanent members of the bureaucracy past and present, this book discerns a pattern of executive implementation of export controls.

2. THE ORIGINS OF THE U.S. EXPORT CONTROL SYSTEM, 1949–1969

THE executive and its institutions are *potentially* autonomous actors. Whether they actually behave autonomously depends in the first instance on their relations to their society, the nature of the challenges they perceive, and the internal structure and shared norms which make up the executive. This chapter considers the configuration of executive-congressional-societal relations, the perceived challenges, and the ideological currents prevailing at the inception of the U.S. export control regime. Executive capacity in export control policymaking and policy implementation in the 1970s and 1980s, as well as the content of the executive's policies and its institutional procedures, can be traced in large measure to the forces and interests of earlier decades.

The establishment of the U.S. peacetime export control system can be linked to prevailing ideology, the U.S. position within international political and economic hierarchies, and the alignment of particular domestic interests. Viewed from an ideological perspective, postwar export controls were anomalous to the prevailing liberal worldview.[1] Shortly after World War II, the United States, after some initial reluctance, fostered a liberal international economic order founded on international law and on institutions such as the GATT, the IMF, and the International Bank for Reconstruction and Development. United States export controls, however, represent a unilateral, artificial, politically motivated barrier to free trade. Thus their development in the late 1940s is, in one sense, a decidedly illiberal component in a fundamentally liberal, free-trade regime. The ideological basis for export controls was, however, an equally powerful competing ideology: anticommunism.

In addition to the ideological motivation of U.S.-Soviet rivalry, the U.S. hegemonic position in the international economy made export controls a viable policy. The United States emerged from the war in a position of unchallenged economic authority. Its willingness to exercise its authority and its resort to export controls were facilitated not only by the country's strength but by the traditional insignificance of foreign trade as a component of American gross national product relative to other Western nations and by the particular insignificance of U.S. trade with Eastern Europe and the Soviet Union. The United States' primary economic concern after World War II continued to be its internal market, despite the absolute importance of its role in international trade and financial markets.

Thus, a structural explanation suggests that export controls were a natural outgrowth of America's relative power position after World War II. As a nation of preponderant power, the United States sought, in addition to free trade, a means to ensure the maintenance of its strategic, technological, and military superiority and domestic stability. Structurally, export controls were a cost—the provision of a collective security good—paid primarily by the United States to maintain a liberal international economic order during a time of severe U.S.-Soviet rivalry. The emergence of a nuclear duopoly shortly thereafter reinforced this structural imperative.

A bureaucratic politics or interest-group explanation emphasizes the domestic factors that led to export controls. In this framework peacetime export controls were the continuation of bureaucratic institutions established during the war whose subsequent operation reflected a balancing of bureaucratic interests among the State, Commerce, and Defense departments. Further, trade controls instituted for strategic purposes were part of a compromise reached between those elements within the domestic society that feared Soviet expansion and those interest groups that sought a more liberal system of world trade.

Taken together, these explanations satisfactorily account for the origin of America's export control system. However, these approaches, while necessary, are not sufficient explanations for the subsequent operation and effect of this system. Once established, the legal and bureaucratic apparatus of the executive influenced policymaking and outcomes as an important, relatively autonomous political actor.

This chapter considers the combination of factors which gave rise to the U.S. export control system. It maintains that, fundamentally, the executive and its domestic and international environments were in accord on export control policy during the 1950s and 1960s.[2] Subsequent chapters will argue that, beginning in the late 1960s, the executive diverged to a greater degree from Congress and domestic interest groups than it did in this earlier period. Nevertheless, the events and ideologies of the early period left a lasting imprint on institutional orientations and practices that influenced the way the executive's institutions shaped policy.

This chapter will also present the basic legal and institutional structure of U.S. export controls.

■ The Export Control Act of 1949

American peacetime export control laws are a relatively recent phenomenon. The current policy of controlling goods and technology not directly used in war dates to before World War II.[3] In 1940, following the German conquest of France, Congress gave the President authority to control or curtail exports of munitions and related items and impose penalties for violations.[4] Two years later Congress expanded this authority to include "any articles, technical data, materials, or supplies."[5] After the war, Congress continued this nascent export control system from year to year until codifying it in the Export Control Act of 1949, the first comprehensive and continuing U.S. peacetime legislation for export restriction.[6]

In the years between the war's end and the passage of the 1949 act, the executive concluded that broadly applied peacetime export controls were an indispensable component of U.S. policy toward the Soviet Union. For example, in December 1947, the National Security Council (NSC) determined that "U.S. national security requires the immediate termination, for an indefinite period, of shipments from the United States to the U.S.S.R. and its satellites ... which would contribute to Soviet military potential."[7] The NSC directive was translated into regulations which prohibited the shipment of goods of direct and indirect military significance destined for the Soviet Union or Eastern Europe. The intent of the policy was "to inflict the greatest economic injury to the U.S.S.R. and its satellites,"[8] and its effect was to drastically reduce the volume of East-West trade.

The Export Control Act of 1949 continued these policies, embargoing particular exports of industrial materials to the Soviet Union and other communist countries. The act authorized the President to "prohibit or curtail" all commercial export of "any articles, materials or supplies, including technical data, except under such rules and regulations as he shall prescribe." (section 3[a]).[9] Thus, the original grant of authority encompassed goods of both direct and indirect military utility. Congress authorized the President to delegate to those executive agencies concerned with the domestic and foreign policy aspects of trade the power to determine which articles to control and which destinations should be denied licensable goods or technologies (section 3[b]).

The stated purposes of the 1949 act were to use export controls to (1) prevent domestic economic shortages (short supply controls); (2) protect national security; and (3) promote the foreign policy of the United States.[10] Immediately following the war, export restrictions may have been necessary to ensure an adequate domestic supply of certain commodities needed at home and made scarce by the war, and to channel particular goods to our allies to assist them in their postwar recovery.[11] These controls were also motivated in large part, however, by an underlying national security concern. Senator Leo Allen (R-Ill.) described the purposes of the 1949 act in the following way:

> In the first place, our domestic situation is strengthened, especially through the curbing of inflationary tendencies caused by foreign demand. And in regard to our security, the program will act as a two-edge sword; we can limit the flow of goods to nations that we suspect are unfriendly and we can see to it that the goods we send to the friendly nations do not find their ultimate destination in the hands of our potential enemies.[12]

Moreover, the short supply motivation for the continuation of export restrictions was soon alleviated by America's expanding economy. The perceived threat of the expanding political and military influence of the Soviet Union, however, is reflected in the legislative history of the Export Control Act and by the political events surrounding the expansion of American export control law.

For example, in late 1948 a Senate committee, investigating the administration of export controls, stated that "the national security aspects of our export control program are of transcendent importance, particularly in view of the present activities of the Soviet Union and its satellites."[13] The findings that accompanied the actual legislation explicitly state that "in the light of the growing concern of democratic nations over the policies of the Eastern

European nations, it is quite clear that our national security requires the exercise of such controls. . . ."[14]

Furthermore, the passage of the Export Control Act followed upon the Truman Doctrine of March 1947, made in response to the establishment of Communist regimes in the Soviet-occupied states of Eastern Europe, Soviet pressure on Iran and Turkey, and the outbreak of civil war in Greece. The Communist overthrow of the government of Czechoslovakia in February 1948 and the Soviet establishment of the Berlin blockade in June of that year solidified impressions that the Soviet Union would be a permanent peacetime threat to U.S. interests.[15] In April 1949, the treaty establishing the North Atlantic Treaty Organization (NATO) for regional defense was signed by the United States and Western allies, and in the same year the United States organized the multilateral Coordinating Committee (COCOM), consisting of Japan and the NATO states except Iceland, in an effort to govern strategic exports to the Soviet bloc.[16] This informal multilateral organization constructed a commodity control list and an exception review process designed to enlist the voluntary participation of member states in controlling the export of militarily significant goods and technology to the Eastern bloc.

When COCOM was established it reflected America's policy preferences and American economic hegemony. While the formulation of COCOM in 1949 was completed in secret, it is known that the United States enlisted the cooperation first of Britain and France and eventually of other European nations despite European legal and political reservations.[17] Responding to what it perceived as a monolithic Communist structure confronting the free world in 1949–50, Congress established America's export control system and encouraged (although not formally including it in U.S. law at that time) the cooperation of Western Europe and Japan in withholding certain goods and commodities from Communist countries through COCOM. Although cooperation was enlisted, it should not be assumed that our allies shared our interest in trade control. Representative Gary Brown (R-Mich.) described Europe's position in the following manner:

> our free world friends and allies at that time were recuperating from the ravages of war; were being fed back to life by the Marshall plan; and were little concerned about export policy, strategic or otherwise, since they had little or not [sic] capacity to compete for export markets. . . . It is obvious that friends

and allies at that time saw no reason at all for not restricting trade in certain items with the Soviet Bloc nations when we were the only nation capable of such trade and we were advocating such restrictions. In other words, when there was no economic interest or benefit to protect or promote in such trade, our friends and allies were quite content to support our posture regarding trade restrictions.[18]

In short, American-sponsored export controls secured allied cooperation through the enormous economic leverage the U.S. trade and aid policies exerted in the years immediately following the Second World War and reflected the "shape of the times both for our nation and for our friends and allies."[19]

The Export Control Act was renewed in 1951, coterminous with the U.S. entry into the Korean War.[20] Congress passed the Mutual Defense Assistance Control Act, known generally as the Battle Act, in that year. The Battle Act permitted the U.S. government to embargo shipments of arms, ammunition, implements of war, nuclear materials, petroleum, and other strategic items to nations where such items would threaten the security of the United States, and it prohibited military, economic, or financial assistance to any nation in violation of the act.[21] The Battle Act was the United States' first statutory attempt to enforce a united allied effort to embargo strategic exports. Its stated purpose was to impose controls and seek multilateral cooperation in controlling products "to oppose and offset by nonmilitary action acts which would threaten the United States and the peace of the World."[22] The act also contained the first statutory authorization for U.S. participation in COCOM.[23] In 1954, Congress enacted the Mutual Security Act, which placed control over the export of arms, ammunition, and other implements of war under the auspices of the Department of State.[24]

■ Institutional Origins and Implementation

The executive used the extremely broad grants of legislative authority contained in the 1949 Export Control Act to place within the Commerce Department a relatively autonomous administrative group called the Office of Export Control which, under various names, had operated similar controls to ensure the availability of supplies during World War II and in the immediate postwar period.

Original authority for the control of exports before and during World War II had been vested in several special agencies. In 1940, the President created an independent Administrator of Export Controls.[25] During the period 1941–44, the President transferred the administrator's functions to a series of agencies for purposes of economic defense and warfare.[26] In 1945, export control authority came to rest in the Commerce Department, whose authority in turn was subdelegated by the Secretary of Commerce to the Office of International Trade (OIT).[27]

The relocation of the Office of Export Control—a wartime institution dedicated to restricting exports injurious to the national defense and foreign policy interests—within the Commerce Department's Office of International Trade can best be considered ironic.[28] OIT lacked peacetime experience in operating export controls, and its function collided directly with the principal function of other Commerce Department agencies: to foster and promote international trade.[29]

The Office of Export Control issued regulations listing which commodities should be controlled, granted or denied applications for export licenses, and investigated violations of its regulations or of the Export Control Act itself. The office established an elaborate system of export licensing to implement its objectives. But, because it lacked experience in this area, internal techniques of administration developed slowly, ad hoc, and by trial and error.

Although the Commerce Department played the lead role in administration, the 1949 act laid the groundwork for multiagency implementation of its provisions. The act required that the Commerce Department seek "information and advice from the several executive departments and independent agencies concerned with our domestic and foreign policies and operations having an important bearing on exports."[30] Early on, the Commerce Department came to consult with the Defense Department for the national security point of view and with the State Department for foreign policy input.[31]

Institutionally, the Office of Export Controls interpreted its initial mandate as requiring the embargo of exports of goods and technology to the Soviet Union, its allies, and "Communist China." This policy was the peacetime continuation of economic warfare; trade was a weapon, and virtually all goods and technologies were to be denied to the potential adversaries of the United States and the West. Although never articulated by the implementing agencies, their approach to export controls was founded on the belief that any East-West trade is a net gain for the Soviet bloc and a net loss for the United States.[32] The approach assumed irreconcilable enmity between the United States and the Soviet bloc and Soviet bloc dependence on trade with the United States for its technological and economic development. The approach adopted a "resource-freeing" understanding of trade and comparative advantage, i.e., trade allows a country to specialize in what it produces most efficiently given its factor endowments and thus to reach its fullest economic (and military) potential.[33] Although the rationale for controlling exports would evolve, albeit less so in executive institutions than in Congress, it will be seen that the Commerce Department and the agencies it consulted carried with them the influence of this original orientation.[34]

The Export Control Act did not impose organizational structures or procedures on the implementing agencies. Nonetheless, since 1949, the daily regulation of exports has been handled in a relatively consistent manner by the bureaucracy. Perhaps the foremost enduring characteristic of the export licensing system is the one-at-a-time, case-by-case method of examining individual applications to export particular goods to particular destinations.[35] Every commodity or technology proposed for export is examined by the Commerce Department, and often formally or informally cleared by other agencies as well. Rather than identifying the potential strategies of countries posing threats and deducing which goods or technologies have a high utility in the service of those strategies, the export control system attempts to identify which goods and technologies are intrinsically more strategic than others and determine if their export to a given destination should be permitted.[36] A system based on such incremental decisions and precedent has remained essentially unchanged for over forty years.

The prevailing concern of the implementing agencies, then and now, has been with identifying if a good or technology is strategic and should be controlled. As David Baldwin has noted, the administrative agencies' analytic principles for determining the strategic quality of goods and technologies have not changed.[37] Moreover, throughout this period the implementing agencies have viewed as paramount the need to control strategic goods and technologies and have treated as inconsequential the effect of an export on U.S. economic strength.

A second enduring feature of the export control system is the multiagency, multilayered review and clearance process. Since 1949, the standard operating procedure for clearing many license applications has involved formal or informal consultation between the Commerce Department and those agencies which possess technical or political expertise relevant to the proposed export. The Departments of State and Defense have been the primary consultants. Other departments and agencies that have often contributed to license decision-making include the Department of Energy, the Central Intelligence Agency, and the National Security Council.

Complex cases have been resolved through an interagency Operating Committee. The Operating Committee is a senior staff-level group composed of career officials from all the major participating agencies (and a number of minor ones), chaired by the Commerce Department representative. The Operating Committee resolves disputes over particular license applications and determines whether a commodity should be included on or deleted from the list of controlled goods.

A voting rule of unanimity prevails in the Operating Committee, creating the possibility of an impasse, rewarding intransigence as a negotiating strategy, and occasionally escalating decisions to the next level of interagency review, where similar decision-making rules apply.[38] The interagency review process is secret, making it difficult for an exporter to identify which agency is delaying its license application.

Lengthy processing times for contentious licensing applications were an early outgrowth of this system. Until the early 1970s, however, there were no statutory or regulatory deadlines on the processing of export licenses. For the first twenty years of the system's operation, the implementing agencies considered it their prerogative to determine when a decision should be made. Delays were justified as necessary for careful consideration of matters touching upon U.S. national security; impatient exporters were reminded that, in view of the danger to national security of an incorrect decision, if a choice were forced, the only administratively acceptable solution would be to deny the proposed export. A persistent lack of personnel and budgetary resources to handle the heavy caseload of the key bureaucracies also contributed to delay.[39]

■ Executive, Congressional, and Interest Group Congruence

At its inception, the export control system was generally consistent with the functional needs of society, the preferences of most political leaders, and the country's basic political beliefs. It maintained this general congruence throughout the 1950s and into the early 1960s. This reference to congruence is not to suggest that differences of degree did not exist between the executive and Congress over export control policy. Nonetheless, laws and nascent institutions reflected, with little distortion, the collective sentiments of American society and the nation's position in the international system. In addition, the bureaucracy's implementation of the Export Control Act accorded with the congressional design, and there is little indication that the act, as written or as applied, contradicted the wishes of the President.

For example, interbranch harmony prevailed during the early years. The expansive peacetime authority and discretion given to the executive to control exports were not matters of major concern to Congress. As noted in Bruce Jentleson's study of East-West energy trade, the prevailing view and tenor of the era was best articulated by Representative Eldon Spence (D-Ky.), who managed the floor debate on the Export Control Bill of 1949:

> Why should we not give the President these powers? We are not in normal times. Times have not been normal since 1940, when he was given these powers. I do not think it would be a good policy to put shackles on the President. . . . In these highly important international affairs, he ought to have the same powers as the executives or dictators representing the enslaved peoples in totalitarian governments. We have got to trust these powers to somebody, and to limit them and restrict them by unnecessary conditions would weaken the very purpose for which they are given.[40]

Similar attitudes were expressed in committee hearings accompanying the passage of the 1949 act.[41]

Furthermore, the years immediately preceding and following the passage of the act were relatively free of interbranch contention over the national security and foreign policy purposes to be served through the use of stringent export controls. During the four years immediately before passage of the Export Control Act, six House committees considered the subject of export control. Only three of those, two of them study committees, explored the basic foreign policy implications of export control policy, and none raised serious doubts as to the need to control trade to the Eastern bloc. After the outbreak of war in Korea, the need for U.S. export controls was so apparent and approval so widely shared in Congress that the House devoted only two minutes to approving a two-year extension of the act.[42]

Finally, by 1949 export controls for national security purposes did not meet with significant domestic political opposition[43] and, in this sense, were reasonably consistent with pluralist understandings of policymaking as well. This claim of a domestic political consensus on the need for export controls is not an assertion that all quarters of American society endorsed them with equal degrees of enthusiasm. Nonetheless, in testimony before Congress, American export industries—the group with the most to lose from export controls—publicly supported strict legislation. For example, Thomas Ballagh, Export Sales Manager of the trading company Ballagh and Thrall, stated in testimony before the Senate: "Whatever the decision of Congress and the OIT, I and my firm, of course, stand ready to cooperate toward the efficient operation of such controls as are determined to be in the best interests of the United States."[44] In testimony before the same committee, William S. Swingle, Executive Vice President of the National Foreign Trade Council, Inc., recognized that export controls were required to fulfill the purposes of U.S. foreign policy.[45] Similarly, in testimony before the House Banking and Currency Committee, Clarence R. Miles of the United States Chamber of Commerce noted that "national security is of paramount importance and the safeguarding of that security is the major reason for the continuation of export controls on highly strategic materials and industrial items to particular areas...."[46]

The attitude of American exporters toward the new law was perhaps best summarized by Joseph A. Sinclair, Secretary, Commerce and Industry Association of New York, Inc. Sinclair, speaking on behalf of approximately 2,000 firms directly interested in international trade, stated:

> Most foreign traders recognized the necessity for a continuation of export controls under present international economic and political conditions, although, with the exception of a few who have actually profited as a result of such controls, American exporters believe that export licensing should be instituted and maintained only when absolutely necessary to carry out our international commitments and for the political and economic security of the country.[47]

Moreover, business groups, sensitive to the prevailing public anticommunist sentiment, not only refrained from opposing the embargo on East-West trade but often publicly voiced their opposition to such trade throughout the 1950s.[48]

Business's publicly stated objections to export controls involved primarily the bureaucratic difficulties they had encountered with export licensing. Louis I. Freed, Executive Secretary of the Independent Merchant Exporters Associated, told a Senate subcommittee:

> This association does not appear in opposition to the principles enunciated in this bill. We recognize the need for a continuation of limited export controls. We agree with Secretary of Commerce Sawyer, who stated before this committee that no public or trade opposition to S. 548 is apparent. There is, however, considerable opposition to the administrative implementation of the announced objectives of this legislation, as evidenced during the past year, and apparently contemplated for the future.[49]

Some businessmen traced their difficulties to the broad delegation of authority granted to the Commerce Department and the lack of legislative guidance as to the administration of the law.[50]

In short, by the end of the Korean War and the advent of the Mutual Security Act, the reasons for maintaining a system of export controls for national security and ideological purposes were entrenched. By that time the short supply controls were used infrequently; the strategic imperative of controls was justified "wholly in terms of foreign policy, and their severity fluctuated with successive international crises and accommodations."[51]

■ Export Control Policy in the 1960s

By the 1960s, the systematic use of export control laws was an accepted foreign policy weapon. A 1961 congressional investigation into the operation of the Export Control Act concluded that the act, as administered, established long and comprehensive lists of controlled commodities covering items of both military and economic significance. Not surprisingly, licenses to ship these commodities were routinely granted when the end users were in the "free world" and routinely rejected for Communist destinations.[52]

A select committee on export controls was chaired by Representative Paul Kitchen (D-N.C.), who zealously believed that a total embargo on U.S. trade with Communist countries was the proper goal to be served by U.S. export controls.[53] Under the impetus of the Kitchen Committee report, in 1962 Congress enacted a series of amendments to the Export Control Act that reaffirmed its mandate to embargo. Congress explicitly authorized the President to consider the "economic significance" of unrestricted export of materials as well as their potential military significance in determining whether an export might adversely affect the security of the United States.[54] Further, the President was empowered to deny export licenses for any item "to any nation or combination of nations threatening the national security of the United States, if the President shall determine that such export makes a significant contribution to the military *or economic* potential of such nations or nations which would prove detrimental to the nation's security *and welfare* of the United States" (emphasis added).[55]

These amendments reflected a continuing, expansive congressional delegation to the executive which provided explicitly that the export of nonmilitary items that assist the economic development of unfriendly nations could be controlled for either national security or foreign policy purposes.[56] Congress made its directive explicit in the report accompanying the amendments:

> The committee emphasizes the fact that the act gives the President the widest possible discretion to limit, restrict, or prohibit entirely exports to any person or to any nation of any or all commodities or articles whether or not, and to whatever extent they are of military, industrial, or economic significance, if limitation, restriction or prohibition is found to be in the interest of our national security or our foreign policy or necessary because of domestic shortages. *The act is not limited to strategic materials or to critical materials or to essential commodities.* It will support a total embargo or the mildest of restrictions. *The requirements of foreign policy, national security and domestic shortages are the only test.* [Emphasis added.][57]

The passage of the 1962 amendment came after President Kennedy's January 30, 1961, State of the Union address in which he expressed his interest in "using economic tools . . . to help reestablish historic ties of friendship" between the United and Soviet Union in situations "clearly in the national interest."[58] Nevertheless, the rhetorical or practical importance of the 1962 amendment in contradicting the executive's wishes should not be overestimated.

Michael Mastanduno's analysis of this period suggests that the 1962 amendment was an example of a congressional declaration of policy that differed significantly from the executive's attitude and marked the beginning of a period in which the executive was less successful in its struggle with Congress over export control policy and instruments.[59] While there may be some truth to this assertion, especially when this period is compared to the post-1969 period in which executive dominance was more clear-cut and dramatic, it is probable that the differences between Congress and the executive in the 1960s were slight and the executive's discretion in the use of export controls remained virtually unfettered throughout the period.[60]

First, President Kennedy's interest in expanding trade with the East as a means of improving relations was moderated, if not extinguished, by the Vienna summit and the Berlin and Cuban crises of 1961–62. Consistent with this interpretation was the Kennedy administration's willingness to embargo the sale of oil pipeline and pipelaying equipment to the Soviet Union and its efforts to pressure the COCOM allies to cancel their pipeline exports and future contracts for Soviet oil in 1961–63. Bruce Jentleson's detailed discussion of the Kennedy pipeline embargo led him to conclude that Congress and the executive continued to share the basic Cold War consensus on export control policy of the early 1950s. In short, Jentleson states, "A decade later little had changed."[61]

Moreover, it should not be assumed that the 1962 congressional statement of commitment to limiting trade that could contribute to the economic well-being of the Soviet bloc was translated into any meaningful limitation on executive institutions' policymaking. The amendment simply confirmed long-standing institutional practice of denying export of a wide range of products for reasons of national security. Mastanduno concedes that after passage of the 1962 amendment, "the Executive still retained considerable discretion in the determination of which items would meet the control criteria."[62] This discretion was so considerable that the Commerce Department representative on the interagency Operating Committee that approved or denied contentious license applications could recall only one instance in his entire tenure when denial of a commodity or technology had to be justified because it contributed to the "economic" as opposed to "military" potential of the Soviet bloc.[63] Moreover, as Mastanduno notes, when the Kennedy administration supported a particular East-West transaction it did not consider the 1962 amendment a hindrance:

> [Executive] discretion was exercised most dramatically in 1963, when the Kennedy administration allowed and publicly supported, a $140 million grain sale to the Soviets. The sale arguably contributed significantly to the economic potential of the Soviets. . . .[64]

In sum, the early 1960s saw no major change in export control policy and no major divergences in congressional-executive attitudes. What initiatives were taken evinced some recognition of the economic benefits of expanded trade and embodied some limited relaxation of national-security-based export controls.

In the mid-1960s, President Johnson expressed some interest in increasing trade with the Soviet Union. Toward this end, a Special Committee on U.S. Trade Relations with East European countries and the Soviet Union was established, composed of representatives of business, labor, and finance. The committee did not propose any liberalization in East-West trade, nor were specific recommendations made in regard to export control laws. The committee favored authorizing the President to grant or deny Most Favored Nation status to individual Eastern bloc nations and concluded that trade with Communist countries should neither be subsidized nor receive undue encouragement.[65]

President Johnson's initiatives were limited to decontrolling some nonstrategic items in October 1966.[66] He also twice submitted to Congress (in 1965 and 1966) an East-West trade relations bill, which would have provided for presidential negotiations on peaceful trade pacts with Communist countries and would have authorized the President to negotiate Most Favored Nation treatment for the products of the country under the agreement. Because of a lack of congressional interest and the preoccupation with the Vietnam War, no hearings were ever held on the bill, and the President never pressed Congress for serious consideration of the proposal.

■ Conclusion

From the years immediately following the Second World War through the mid-1960s, Congress and the executive pursued a common policy of embargoing most trade with Communist countries. Throughout this period the interests of the executive, Congress, and domestic interest groups were essentially in accord.

A unique combination of factors had spawned and shaped the U.S. export control system and created a strong, insulated, and procedurally complex executive apparatus for the control of exports for reasons of national security and foreign policy. The executive and its bureaucracy, by the authority of the Export Control Act, used the export control system primarily as a Cold War tool to impose a limited embargo against Communist states. For two decades the executive, Congress, and domestic business groups remained fundamentally in harmony on the goals and operation of export controls, and the executive and executive institutions were seldom seriously questioned.

3. EXPORT CONTROL LAW AND POLICY IN THE 1970s

THE passage of the Export Administration Act of 1969 marked a turning point in the congressional attitude toward export controls. A majority in Congress, responding to changed economic conditions and particular domestic interests, attempted to liberalize policy as a means of expanding American exports. Looking back over America's export policy and its premises in the late 1960s, the U.S. Senate proclaimed that "virtually every circumstance which made the Export Control Act both advisable and feasible has changed."[1] In particular, Congress expressed its awareness that the Soviet Union could either manufacture products that met its own needs or purchase what it needed from other nations. Moreover, Congress noted that tensions between the United States and the Soviet Union had lessened, and that it was imperative that the United States improve its declining balance-of-payments position.

Congress's major attempts at reform included efforts to: (1) limit the number of commodities subject to control for national security reasons; (2) instill a recognition within the executive that the foreign availability of a controlled commodity should be weighed by the bureaucracy in granting licenses; (3) make the licensing process more open and accountable to the business community; and (4) harmonize the practices of the United States with those of its allies through the multilateral coordinating committee known as COCOM. In short, the new 1969 act provided that export licenses could be denied only if a product would contribute significantly to a potential enemy's military capability, and then only if no comparable product could be obtained from a foreign supplier.

There are times, however, when the executive's interest conflicts with interests of societal groups or Congress. It is at these times that central "state" actors more clearly define, as Krasner has phrased it, "the national interest—the goals the state pursues."[2] The executive branch did not share the congressional enthusiasm for expanding East-West trade. Initially the executive opposed any relaxation in export controls. Its attitude would not change until three years later when, after securing certain concessions from the Soviet Union and in the interests of détente, the Nixon administration did express an interest in expanding East-West trade. At the time of the 1969 bill, however, the President decreed that his appointees in the relevant departments should uniformly oppose each of the attempted congressional reforms. In general, the executive placed greater emphasis than Congress on the national security and foreign policy purposes served by the existing system. The executive also fought to maintain its prerogative in the use and administration of export controls so that policy could be fashioned by the executive without the hindrance of legislative reforms.

The first part of this chapter will demonstrate that the executive articulated a different policy from that of the congressional majority and lobbied successfully for language in the 1969 act that turned many of the proposed reforms into recommendations which ensured executive primacy in policymaking. The second half will demonstrate that the four major reforms sought by Congress were blunted, delayed, or ignored, in whole or in part, through the executive's implementation of the 1969 act.

Under the act the method of implementing policy continued to be left largely to the executive's discretion. The President delegated primary authority to the Commerce Department to review the list of restricted items and technology, to make changes in accordance with U.S. policy, and to process license applications in consultation with other relevant agencies. Consequently, executive departments that would administer the 1969 act were the same offices that for two decades administered its predecessor. Embedded institutional practices and certain bureaucratic decisions would lead to greater burdens on U.S. exporters than those intended by Congress or anticipated by the business community and COCOM nations.

■ The Export Administration Act of 1969

The late 1960s were a period of reassessment of U.S. export policies. Although Congress remained intent on banning the export of materials and technologies that could make a "significant contribution to the military potential" of Communist countries,[3] conditions had changed and new interests had emerged that seriously undermined the effectiveness of the Export Control Act. The need for revision of existing legislation became increasingly sharp.

One significant change involved a restructuring of the international economic hierarchy. The United States's economic power relative to Western Europe and Japan had declined since the post–World War II era, and international trade had assumed a more important position in the American economy. It became apparent to Congress that the role of the United States as the primary supplier of industrial and strategic goods had diminished and that many goods and technologies restricted by U.S. export control laws were available to the Soviet Union from other sources or could be produced by the Soviets themselves.[4] In a Senate floor debate on the Export Administration Bill of 1969, Senator Walter Mondale (D-Minn.) acknowledged that

> economic warfare may result in exactly the opposite of the intended effect. By withholding trade, we encourage a nation to develop its own resources, . . . forcing the creation of a new industrial capacity to produce the item denied.[5]

The degree of allied cooperation and adherence to the COCOM list of restricted items had declined as well. The House Subcommittee on International Trade noted that in 1968 the United States controlled 2,029 commodity categories for export to such countries as Bulgaria, Czechoslovakia, Hungary, and the Soviet Union, and 1,753 categories for Poland and Romania, while in that year COCOM had designated 552 categories for control. The subcommittee's chairman, Representative Thomas L. Ashly (D-Ohio), characterized the U.S. approach to export controls as "compulsory" and chastised U.S. policy for failing to distinguish between strategic and nonstrategic goods as COCOM allies did.[6]

In its decision to rewrite the Export Control Act, Congress was also responding to new business demands for access to markets. By 1969, the business community was expressing a strong interest in competing with foreign firms in previously inaccessible East European markets and was chafing against the export restrictions established by the act.[7] Hewlett-Packard Corporation was one of many U.S. firms concerned with the 1969 revisions. In testimony before the House Subcommittee on International Trade, Thomas A. Christiansen, manager of Hewlett-Packard's International Planning Division, explained that his firm anticipated that its international sales would double by 1975. While sales to Eastern Europe currently accounted for less than 1 percent of its international sales volume, Hewlett-Packard felt it could no longer afford to ignore the rapidly growing East European market. The most important factor Christiansen cited as limiting market expansion was "the high level of unilaterally imposed U.S. export controls." He added, "controls of this type, not imposed on West European and Japanese manufacturers, adversely affect our ability to compete in East European markets."[8]

The Senate Committee on Banking and Currency, which took the lead in drafting the 1969 bill, was sympathetic to the business community's interests. Senator Harrison Williams (D-N.J.), a majority member of that committee, noted:

> At this date, virtually every United States product finds one or more competitor products being produced by our allies. And, our allies do not deny themselves the trade with Eastern Europe that we do. Consequently, by denying Eastern Europe United States products we no longer deny them access to the goods and technology from one of our allies. Thus, the only group being denied anything is American business; it is being denied the right to sell its products in a competitive market which is expanding and becoming more competitive every year. Coming at a time when we are experiencing serious trade balance difficulties, it just doesn't make sense to ignore such a market because of outdated ineffective policies.[9]

Congress perceived the business sector's interest in expanding markets as an opportunity to increase domestic employment while improving the U.S. balance-of-payments position. In contrast to the immediate postwar years, in which the United States had a very large balance-of-payments surplus, by 1969 the U.S. surplus had decreased sharply. Congress felt it necessary to take steps to increase the U.S. trade surplus by expanding exports to the Eastern bloc "unless some other real and overriding national objective would be served" by maintaining restrictions.[10]

Congress also sensed at this time an easing in East-West tensions which would facilitate its passage of a more liberal export control bill. The Senate Committee on Banking and Currency recognized that the United States was "attempting to enter a new phase in its dealings with Russia and Eastern Europe—a phase which will hopefully bring about even greater improvements in our relations with those countries than we have witnessed in recent years."[11] The committee added that it was convinced that liberalization of trade restrictions could be an extremely effective means of bringing about greater understanding between the United States and these nations.[12]

The Export Administration Act of 1969 reflected Congress's perceptions of these changes and represented an important departure in both tone and substance from the Export Control Act. There were, of course, differences of opinion within Congress on the need to reform U.S. export controls. The minority Senate position did not perceive the need for the new legislation.[13] Further, the bill initially passed by the House contained only modest liberalizations.

Ultimately, the House bill and the more liberal Senate bill were sent to a conference committee, from which emerged, on November 4, a bill embodying most of the Senate's proposed changes. Although the bill quickly won approval in the Senate, the House rejected the conference report, 157–238, with Republicans opposing it 5–171.

House defeat of the conference bill was attributable largely to the administration's staunch opposition. The administration marshaled House Republican opposition before the vote when Secretary of Commerce Maurice Stans wrote a strong letter of opposition to Representative William B. Widall (R-N.J.), the ranking Republican on the House Banking and Currency Committee. Stans's letter cited numerous administration objections and asked that the conference bill be amended. The letter was read on the House floor as that chamber was considering the conference report.

The House then sent the bill back to the Senate with an amendment undoing many of the Senate's proposed liberalizations. With two days remaining in the session, the House and Senate reopened negotiations, and an agreement was reached on the morning of the session's final day.

Nonetheless, the 1969 act represented a change in the congressional focus of American export control policy from a strategic embargo seeking to limit East-West trade toward a policy of qualified free trade seeking to promote exports that did not endanger national security. Congress again called for exports restrictions only: to protect the economy from the excessive drain of scarce materials and to reduce the serious inflationary impact of foreign demand; to further the foreign policy of the United States and fulfill its international responsibilities; and to ensure national security. Congress sought to allow the expansion of East-West trade in recognition of changed conditions without losing sight of the goal of national security. In section 3 of the 1969 act, Congress expressed this dual purpose:

> (A) to encourage trade with all countries with which we have diplomatic or trading relations, except those countries with which such trade has been determined by the President to be against the national interest, and (B) to restrict the export of goods and technology which would make a significant contribution to the military potential of any other nation or nations which would prove detrimental to the national security of the United States.[14]

Congress attempted four major reforms in the 1969 act. First, it directed the executive to limit the number of commodities subject to export controls for national security purposes. The act required the Secretary of Commerce to review any departmental export control lists "with a view to making promptly such changes and revisions in such lists as may be necessary or desirable in furtherance of the policy, purposes, and provisions of this Act."[15] With regard to national security controls, the act lifted the prohibition on the export of goods contributing to the "economic potential" of hostile nations, which had been included in the 1962 amendment, and provided instead that the President could control only the export of articles, materials, supplies, data, or information that would "make a significant contribution to the military potential of such [hostile] nation or nations which would prove detrimental to the national security of the United States...."[16]

Second, Congress recognized that the foreign availability of a controlled commodity should be an important factor weighed by the bureaucracy in granting licenses. Before implementing national security controls, the President was required to determine that the commodities or data regulated were not readily available to involved nations from other sources; if they were readily available and he nonetheless determined that an export restriction was "necessary in the interest of national security," he had to report his reasons to Congress. No such restrictions applied to controls implemented for foreign policy reasons.[17]

Third, Congress sought to make the export licensing process more open and accountable to the business community by requiring the Commerce Department to consult with relevant U.S. producers regarding the scope of the control list and foreign availability assessment, and by subjecting departmental action to judicial review. The Secretary of Commerce was required to report to Congress with regard to Commerce's compliance with the provisions of the 1969 act and to keep the business sector fully apprised of changes in policy and procedure.[18]

Finally, Congress instructed the executive to harmonize to a greater degree the export practices of the United States with those of its allies through COCOM. Congress exhorted the executive agencies to implement the new act "with a view to promoting trade with all nations with which the United States is engaged in trade"[19] through the prompt removal of controls which were unnecessary to protect national security. Congress also sought to persuade the executive branch to harmonize its licensing practices with those of COCOM by encouraging Commerce to conduct the necessary procedural reforms to facilitate trade with the Eastern bloc.

The executive's perceptions differed from those of the congressional majority. The executive—the President and his appointees in the relevant departments—while not averse to expanding American exports, made clear its desire to place priority on the national security and foreign policy purposes of export controls and the maintenance of the executive's prerogative in their use and administration.

In this regard, it is noteworthy that the executive's policy apparently emanated directly from the President and served to unify the legislative stance of the various executive agencies. Early in its administration, the Nixon White House solicited the views of the State, Defense, and Commerce departments on the proper role of East-West trade. National Security Council Director Henry Kissinger forwarded to President Nixon a briefing paper summarizing his and the departments' recommendations which, according to Kissinger, included some liberalization of export controls and an expansion of East-West trade. President Nixon rejected the recommendation, however, and announced that the administration would oppose all legislation aimed at liberalizing East-West trade.[20]

Consequently, the President and the executive departments uniformly supported an extension of the 1949 act then in effect. The Nixon administration proposed an amendment that simply extended the expiration date to June 1973.[21] During hearings on proposed amendments, Acting Assistant Secretary of State Joseph A. Greenwald told the Senate, "this isn't either the time or the circumstances to make what would be a major change."[22]

The executive's actions were consistent with the foreign policy of the Nixon administration, particularly Kissinger's policy toward the Soviet Union at the time. An NSC staff member described the Nixon administration's policy on East-West trade and technology transfer as more cautious than that of the congressional majority. In fact, the Nixon administration believed that Congress's efforts were premature and the "functional equivalent of unilateral disarmament—granting the Soviets access to U.S. goods and technology without extracting anything in return."[23] Others within the administration characterized the Nixon-Kissinger attitude toward East-West trade as realistic: both men believed that East-West trade was not per se good or bad and that American technology should be gradually "rolled out" to the Soviet Union and its allies in exchange for political concessions. Consequently, the Nixon administration viewed the 1969 bill as an example of congressional concessions to parochial business interests which could impede the executive policy of quid pro quo.[24]

Although the executive branch recognized, at least in part, the changing conditions that prompted the congressional attempt to relax export controls, it believed that such a relaxation would have little positive impact on East-West trade and that any trade liberalization should be closely linked to political relations. Here the executive's perspective differed from that of the majority in Congress or interest groups on the goals to be served by U.S. export control policy and the means by which to achieve those goals. Before the 1969 bill was enacted, the executive, in marked contrast to the congressional focus on export expansion, supported measures it believed would further national security and ideological aims and those which would allow the executive the greatest policy flexibility.

The executive's orientation toward export controls was reflected uniformly in testimony of the heads of the relevant executive agencies. For example, in a statement before the Senate Subcommittee on International Finance, Joseph Greenwald summarized the State Department's position:

> We believe that the present act has proved over the years to be a workable formulation of policy and of necessary authority and enforcement. It provides sufficient discretionary power to

permit the President to act flexibly in response to different situations at different times. There is great virtue in such legislation. If the language of the law were more explicit, its versatility in meeting changed circumstances would be less. As it is, the Act has permitted the implementation of policies of total trade denial to certain Communist countries while at the same time permitting policies of continuing to facilitate nonstrategic trade with certain other Communist countries.[25]

Greenwald added that prospects for an increase in nonstrategic trade with Eastern Europe and the Soviet Union would be modest at best under existing conditions. The State Department attributed the limited volume of East-West trade to Eastern Europe's lack of foreign exchange, limited import needs, and the limited appeal of Soviet and East European goods to the American market. The State Department emphasized the political significance of export controls as a signal to the Soviets of U.S. resolve along with its belief that the current status of East-West relations did not merit a uniform trade liberalization.[26]

The Department of Defense spokesman, G. Warren Nutter, Assistant Secretary of Defense, International Security Affairs, in testimony before the House Subcommittee on International Trade stated succinctly:

> As you gentlemen are well aware, there are two fundamental questions involved in any discussion of H.R. 4293 [A Bill to Extend and Amend the Export Control Act of 1949]. First is there a continued need for exercising selective controls over strategic exports to Communist countries? Second, does the Export Control Act in its present form provide for an implementation of national policy that is sufficiently flexible? The Department of Defense, in supporting H.R. 4293, believes that the answer to both questions is yes.[27]

Nutter also cautioned the subcommittee about unduly fettering the President's discretion in foreign affairs and stated that the Defense Department policy "on relaxing export controls should go hand in hand with relaxation of international tension."[28]

The Department of Commerce, which held primary responsibility for the administration of the Export Control Act, echoed the sentiments of the Defense and State departments. Kenneth N. Davis, Assistant Secretary for Domestic and International Business, noted:

In its present form the Act has proved to be flexible enough to permit adaptation to any international developments. Controls can be relaxed or eliminated to meet improved conditions, or conversely, can be imposed or tightened to meet new challenges or worsening conditions. Regardless of whether we wish to relax or strengthen our controls we shall continue to need a control mechanism. Therefore, we believe that the present Act should be extended to permit us to deal effectively with the problems that arise.[29]

The Commerce Department's reiteration of the sentiments of the State and Defense Department and its offering of specific rebuttals to many of the planned congressional reforms is significant. The Commerce Department did not support the interests which the business community had forcefully expressed to Congress. A bureaucratic politics or Marxist/instrumentalist view of policymaking would have predicted a different result; that Commerce, as the bureaucracy most closely related to the business community, would support probusiness legislation.

The executive's general approach to the new legislation was translated into specific opposition to the four major congressional reforms noted above. All three executive departments opposed any limitations on the President's authority to use trade controls for national security purposes. The State, Commerce, and Defense departments flatly opposed the requirement that the executive branch consider the foreign availability of controlled goods in placing or removing commodities from the control list, as well as the requirement that it must justify a decision to control an item either to Congress or, conceivably, to the courts under the Administrative Procedures Act.[30]

The executive departments also made clear their opposition to the congressional recommendation that they give greater consideration to the foreign availability of controlled commodities as a factor in making licensing decisions.[31] The departments opposed the suggestions that business was inadequately informed on agency policy procedures under the existing act and that American licensing policy and practices should coordinate more closely with those of other COCOM countries. Commerce also claimed that its existing policies and procedures were sufficiently responsive to business.[32]

All three departments justified the need to regulate more commodities than were controlled by America's COCOM allies, who regulated only goods and technology of direct military significance. Assistant Secretary of Defense Nutter stated:

> The Defense Department is fully aware of the problems created by our maintaining a commodity control list that is more restrictive than the list of our allies in the coordinating committee [COCOM] . . . our list remains more restrictive for one important reason: because we shoulder the major responsibility in defending the free world. We cannot avoid reckoning with the added cost of defense that accompanies each lowering of restrictions on trade in items of strategic significance. . . .
> Another reason for our more restrictive export controls arises from the fact that our investment in the technology of sophisticated weaponry is far larger than that of our allies. As a matter of practical necessity, we must resolve in our own favor any doubts we may have as to whether we enjoy a technological lead over Communist countries.[33]

The Commerce Department also clearly stated that it intended to control items with both military and civilian applications.[34] The State Department, the agency with direct responsibility for coordination with COCOM, added that because of the U.S. position of controlling strategic and certain nonstrategic items, American licensing policy would necessarily be at "a competitive disadvantage for an American firm as compared with a firm in another Western country" not subject to such licensing restrictions.[35]

With regard to the growing divergence between the United States and allied nations' export control policies, the United States faced two policy alternatives: the United States could pressure American business and America's allies to continue to comply with a more restrictive conception of U.S. export controls than they otherwise would pursue; or the United States could loosen its licensing procedures to increase U.S. exports and align the philosophy and practice of export controls with those of America's allies and the wishes of the domestic business community. It is clear that the executive favored the former approach, whereas Congress favored the latter.

During the legislative process, the executive won important compromises from Congress on several points. Under the final version of the 1969 act, agency and presidential decisions were not subject to judicial review, and the President retained a good deal of flexibility in pursuing national security and foreign policy export controls. The congressional approaches to liberalization through procedures more responsive to business, assessment of foreign availability, and licensing practices more in line with America's COCOM allies essentially were reduced to nonbinding recommendations.

Moreover, the President remained free to choose the purpose for which export controls were to apply and could avoid congressional restraints on the use of national security controls entirely by declaring that a control was implemented for foreign policy as opposed to national security reasons. Further, the President could impose controls for national security purposes even in situations where the goods or technologies were available from foreign sources, provided the reasons for such controls were reported to Congress. Congress also opted to delete from the reform legislation a section providing that the decision to place an item on an export control list be subject to the Administrative Procedures Act, which permits due process and judicial review for executive branch decisions.[36] Hence, an export control decision could only be appealed within the administering agency.

In sum, although Congress amended U.S. export control laws to serve the dual purposes of national security and free trade, the executive reserved the authority to maintain a system of trade controls that could be used for national security, foreign policy, and ideological purposes as the executive chose to define them.

The congressional restraints placed on the President, although earnest, were effectively recommendations. Congress chose to tread lightly to avoid a presidential veto and in recognition of its limitations in managing executive institutions and their practices.

Contemporaneous interpretations of the 1969 act recognized the executive's ability to prevail over Congress (particularly the Senate) in several important aspects of the legislation. The Washington periodical *National Journal* described final passage of the 1969 act as an "administration victory" and noted that under the final version "the President [could] block export of any item, regardless of its availability, if he felt its export would be detrimental to the national security."[37]

Several factors contributed to the executive's ability to prevail during passage of the 1969 act. Foremost, perhaps, were the divisions within Congress on the desirability of export control reform. Although Congress was generally disposed to liberalize the act, the impetus for reform came primarily from the Senate, more particularly from Senate Democrats, and more particularly still from Senate Democrats on the Banking and Currency Committee. A significant minority within Congress was opposed to liberalization. These divisions enhanced the executive's maneuverability in dealing with Congress, which, as an institution, was far less able than the executive to speak with one voice.

Moreover, institutional procedures within Congress made it difficult to sustain momentum for reform. James Sundquist has noted generally that "in the process of overcoming the countless legislative hurdles, policies may be compromised to the point of ineffectiveness."[38] This tendency to compromise is particularly pronounced where, as in 1969, the President takes a position in direct opposition to the congressional demands for change, marshals the loyalty of the relevant bureaucratic agencies in opposing the legislation, and exercises his partisan influence over House members during the final passage of the act.[39] It is also interesting to note the executive's ability to move quickly in galvanizing bureaucratic appointees' opposition to reform—an unexpected result under a bureaucratic politics explanation, which views the executive as hamstrung by internal divisions.

Two additional factors contributed to the executive's legislative effectiveness. First, the executive possessed the technical expertise required to construct or obstruct meaningful reform. Congressional involvement in export controls is episodic and lacks the depth and continuity of the administrative agencies. This informational problem is compounded by the highly technical and scientific data that are part of the export control policymaking process. On a daily basis, the ability to make the technological assessments crucial to export control policy resides within the executive.

Finally, because export control policy is a topic directly related to national security, a congressional challenge to executive prerogative and executive judgment cannot be made without peril. Congress is constrained in some measure by the threat that the executive will brand its efforts to liberalize the laws as reckless and a threat to national security made for certain commercial interests. Although no special interest group exerts this influence, Congress recognizes that the executive can invoke the concerns of the general populace with such an appeal.

■ The Execution of Policy: Export Controls in the 1970s

The President's opposition to expanded East-West trade underwent a reappraisal in the early 1970s—a time in which President Nixon reopened relations (including trade relations) with the People's Republic of China and negotiated, in 1972, an unratified trade agreement with the USSR. The 1972 U.S.-Soviet Trade Agreement failed when Congress, led by Senator Henry Jackson (D-Wash.), linked the granting of Most Favored Nation (MFN) status for the USSR to the improvement of human rights in the Soviet Union and, in particular, to the freedom of Jews and other minority groups to emigrate.[40] Congress eventually passed what became known as the Jackson-Vanik amendment over the opposition of the Nixon and Ford administrations led by Secretary of State Kissinger. Its passage forced the Soviet Union to notify the U.S. government, by letter dated January 10, 1975, that it could not accept a trade agreement which included this amendment.

The MFN episode represents some departure from the general picture of executive-congressional relations given earlier. First, it presents a situation in which the executive more enthusiastically sought expanded East-West trade and Congress pursued a more restrictive trade policy for ideological, i.e., human rights, reasons. Viewed another way, however, this episode is consistent with the general point that the executive possesses a greater interest in national security as the goal to be served by trade and that Congress is more responsive to domestic interest group pressures. In this instance, during the period of détente, the executive perceived American security interests as best served by limited rapprochement with the Soviet Union facilitated by expanded nonstrategic trade. Congress, led by a senatorial minority that traditionally had been skeptical of East-West trade and pressured by domestic human rights and religious groups, proved to be more responsive to these interests groups than the executive. In short, while the executive was pushing for expanded East-West trade in the face of congressional opposition (a reversal of positions established during passage of the 1969 Export Administration Act), this policy position can be seen as consistent with a claim of executive emphasis on national security and congressional emphasis on particular societal interests.[41]

Second, this incident reflects some of the limits that attend executive autonomy and authority vis-à-vis Congress and highly organized interest groups. This exception does not, however, significantly undermine the general thesis regarding executive autonomy in export controls. The Jackson-Vanik amendment enlivened and entangled a number of normally separate foreign policy and domestic issue groups into a coalition led by a strong senator with presidential aspirations. It was a coalition of the left and right and included exceptional actors, such as academic associations concerned with the repression of dissidents in the USSR and a variety of active Jewish organizations and leaders of American Jewry. Such a coalition had never before come together and has not come together since. Furthermore, Michael Mastanduno pointed out, the executive's capacity is affected by the nature and relevance of different policy instruments. In contrasting export control policy with the granting of MFN status, Mastanduno notes that the selective, highly technical, and institutionally operationalized nature of export controls gives the executive a natural advantage over Congress in administration and contributes to the executive's wide discretion, whereas the granting of MFN status is an instrument that lends itself more readily to congressional control; it is a specific benefit that can be granted or not granted to a particular trading partner.[42]

Despite the executive's softening attitude toward expanded nonstrategic trade with the East, the four major reforms sought by Congress in the 1969 act were slowly or incompletely realized. The reason congressional aims went unfulfilled lay initially in the executive's ambivalence; national security was redefined to include expanded, yet still limited, East-West contacts. Also, the executive's failure to adopt a more liberal East-West trade policy until three years after passage of the 1969 act substantially affected its implementation. Subsequently, the institutional implementation of the act also profoundly influenced policy outcomes. Under the 1969 act, the method of implementing policy continued to be left largely to the executive's discretion. The President delegated primary authority to the Commerce Department to review the list of restricted items and technology, to make changes in accord with U.S. policy, and to process license applications. Consequently, the Office of Export Administration of the Department of Commerce, which would administer the 1969 act, was the same office that for two decades had administered the 1949 act and had operated similar controls to ensure the availability of supplies during World War II. Embedded institutional practices, delays in licensing decision-making, and bureaucratic decisions regarding which commodities possessed "military significance" and whether "foreign availability" of controlled commodities made continued licensing impractical maintained burdens on U.S. exporters that were contrary to the hopes of Congress, the business community, and COCOM nations.

The persistent nature of U.S. export control procedures and institutions was summarized by Graham T. Allison in a government study conducted in 1975:

> In the aftermath of World War II, in response to problems of the Cold War, security defined in military terms became the overriding purpose abroad—both in concept and in organizational form. Today, the concept has somewhat changed, but the organizational form mostly remains.[43]

The enduring "organizational form" affected the four congressional initiatives.

Capping the executive's partial success during the lawmaking process was the fact that the discretion given to the executive to implement the congressional purposes and directives enunciated in the act was not altered. Section 4(d) of the 1969 act provided, like its predecessor, that "the President may delegate the power, authority, and discretion conferred upon him by this Act to such departments, agencies, or officials of the Government as he may deem appropriate." This continuing power of delegation was one way of ensuring continuity, rather than change, in export control practices.

Congress's first major reform, the removal of controls on certain commodities and technologies controlled for national security reasons, was delayed for three years because of the executive's independent timetable for East-West trade liberalization. Export controls continued to restrict a host of commodities of questionable strategic importance throughout the early 1970s. Decontrol actions varied a great deal from industry to industry. Most industries saw very few of their products decontrolled. The decontrolled products generally were low-technology items for which foreign demand was limited. For example, the machine tool industry submitted extensive data to the Office of Export Administration showing that many nonstrategic machine tools were readily available from European and Japanese sources. By mid-1972, however, virtually all machine tools, including general purpose tools such as grinders, transfer machines, milling machines, and lathes, remained subject to unilateral U.S. export control.[44]

The continuation of controls was not limited to any specific industry. Chemicals, electrical machinery, other types of machinery including machine tools, and certain types of fabrics and materials were some of the industrial categories subject to unilateral control. A Senate oversight committee believed that many items were controlled because of the executive's "overly cautious" interpretation of what constitutes "significant military applicability" and stated it "would welcome the decontrol of such items."[45]

The Commerce Department made some minimal progress in decontrolling nonmilitary exports in the years immediately following the 1969 enactment. Controls over many technologically unsophisticated products, however, were not lifted until late 1972 or 1973 after the executive embraced détente and pressured the administering agencies to decontrol items for export to the Eastern bloc.[46]

Not until May 29, 1973 did the Commerce Department significantly reduce the number of unilaterally controlled commodities listed on the Commodity Control List (CCL). At that time, Commerce reduced the number of unilaterally controlled commodity categories on the CCL from 550 entries (mainly commodities of limited strategic importance) to 73.[47] Those involved in formulating policy at this time stated that the prior delay was the result of an explicit executive decision to implement export control policy in a more deliberate and more deliberately political manner than that urged by Congress.[48] Moreover, the tendency for the executive to maintain controls on products and technologies long after they became widely available within the Soviet bloc remained a consistent feature of U.S. export control policy. For example, the controls on computers instituted in 1976 remained unchanged for nearly a decade.[49]

Congress's second major reform effort, institutionalizing foreign availability assessment as a licensing criterion, was largely ignored by executive agencies although Congress called for its institutionalization repeatedly in the 1970s and 1980s.[50] While entries were made to, and withdrawn from, the CCL periodically throughout the 1970s, the Commerce Department consistently maintained the right to add or retain commodities under full security controls regardless of foreign availability.

During the 1970s the Commerce Department made little or no progress in establishing a capacity to monitor foreign availability.[51] As late as fiscal years 1980–85, no licenses were granted for reasons of foreign availability, and until 1985 only two Commerce Department employees were assigned to the assessment of foreign availability. In fact, the Commerce Department did not develop formal regulatory guidelines governing such assessment until 1985.[52]

While there is no doubt that Congress's repeated efforts at injecting foreign availability assessment into licensing and list revision were repeatedly ignored, the explanation for the disparity between congressional aspiration and executive implementation is less clear cut. There is no one definitive explanation. Discussions with appointed officials and permanent members of the bureaucracy who served at the Commerce, Defense, and State departments during the 1970s reveal that congressional urgings were considered serious requests by the bureaucracy, but were never implemented for several reasons. Insufficient personnel and expertise, institutional inertia, decentralization of decision-making, and bureaucratic reluctance to admit that some controlled commodities were not only available from foreign sources but so widely available in the United States as to prevent effective enforcement of export restrictions all contributed to the bureaucracy's failure to reform its assessment of foreign availability.[53]

According to one former Commerce Department official, his office believed that foreign availability assessment was impractical, and improving such assessment was not seriously undertaken at the political level within Commerce. Permanent members of the bureaucracy revealed that an explicit policy decision to ignore or slight foreign availability assessment was made by the permanent bureaucracy as well. In short, a decision was made both at the political level and at the level of the permanent bureaucracy to perpetuate a policy at odds with that designed by Congress. The diffusion of the export control process and the exemption from judicial review—prerogatives successfully defended during the passage of the 1969 law—helped ensure that executive institutions were shielded from close scrutiny and not held fully accountable for their failure to institute this reform.

The complexity of the export licensing system, institutional rigidity, and lack of accountability also resulted in licensing delays, unpredictability, and lack of responsiveness to American exporters, notwithstanding Congress's intent to the contrary.[54] By the spring of 1972, during oversight hearings on the 1969 act, Congress recognized that the goal of accountability to business was not being fulfilled. Two and one-half years after passage of the act, the House Committee on Banking and Currency found that the executive's consultation with business was limited because of insufficient agency procedures for consulting with domestic producers who knew the products, the foreign competition, and the "state of the art."[55]

In the Equal Export Opportunity Act of 1972 Congress sought to rectify this continuing lack of consultation. Congress declared that it is the policy of the United States to subject all controls to governmental review in consultation with qualified experts from private industry. To effect this review, the Secretary of Commerce was directed "upon written request by representatives of a substantial segment of any industry which produces ... [commodities] ... subject to export controls ... [to] appoint ... Technical Advisory Committee[s] ... [consisting] of representatives of U.S. industry and Government."[56] These Technical Advisory Committees (TACs) were to be "consulted with respect to questions involving technical matters, worldwide availability, and actual utilization of production and technology and licensing procedures which may affect the level of [unilateral U.S. and COCOM] export controls. ..."[57] As a result of this legislation, the Secretary of Commerce established the following seven TACs: semiconductors; semiconductor manufacturing and test equipment; numerically controlled machine tools; telecommunications equipment; computer systems; computer peripherals, components, and related test equipment; and electronic instrumentation.

In the spring of 1974, Congress again conducted oversight hearings on the subject of export controls and subsequently proposed amending and extending legislation.[58] Included among the various amendments was a provision to strengthen the Joint Business/Government Technical Advisory committees which were to review and suggest changes to the export control regulations. This enhancement of the TACs was to be accomplished by requiring active membership on each committee by representatives of the Departments of Commerce, Defense, State, and other appropriate agencies.[59] In addition, consistent with national security, each TAC was to be supplied with adequate information concerning the reasons for the existing or contemplated export controls.

In practice, these additional congressional reforms did little to respond to American exporters' needs. American business believed that the executive departments essentially ignored or rejected TAC recommendations without further consultation or notification of the TAC involved.[60] Administrators within the Defense, Commerce, and State departments during the period conceded that the effectiveness of the TACs in involving business in export control policy was, at best, limited. One former Defense Department official noted that his department was not opposed to technical input from the business community before or after the creation of the TACs. He added, however, that business's advice on policy matters was never actively solicited by the Defense Department during the 1970s. Furthermore, the effectiveness of the TACs varied greatly; the semiconductor TAC was somewhat effective in funneling business advice and expertise into the system. The computer TAC, in contrast, was largely ineffective, and other TACs deteriorated as a result of decisions by business that their needs were not being served through continued participation.

Part of the failure of the TACs to respond to business's need to participate in export control decision-making and to receive feedback from the relevant agencies stemmed directly from the manner in which the bureaucracy implemented the congressional directive. First, the majority of TAC deliberations were classified, limiting access to much information that business needed to actively and effectively participate in the process. Second, business and industry representatives on the TACs were limited to a two-year term, whereas government members served indefinitely. Business and industry believed that this arrangement "caused disruption and allowed very little time for an individual to become familiar with the other members of the Committee before they are required to step down."[61] Finally, the legislation enabling the TACs specified that they would report to the Secretary of Commerce. The receipt of reports, however, was delegated within the Commerce Department to the Office of Export Administration, an overworked and understaffed processing office with a long history of not wanting or accepting industry input.

An in-depth study of bureaucratic responsiveness, conducted by the General Accounting Office in 1978,[62] concluded that the congressional aspiration for greater institutional accountability was not met largely because the institutional structures and procedures made accountability impossible. The study concluded:

> With the current licensing system, several organizations within OEA [Office of Export Administration] as well as the consulting departments and agencies of the export licensing community share management responsibility for some export license applications. This diffusion of authority makes it difficult for exporters to communicate meaningfully with their government about export licensing and this difficulty in turn adds needless uncertainty to the export business.[63]

The report recommended that the licensing system should be revised to strike a balance between the need for greater accountability and the government's responsibility to control exports for national security, foreign policy, and short supply reasons. The GAO added that management of export licensing by many agencies and offices within the executive branch was the main obstacle to achieving this balance.[64]

In implementing the congressional aim of aligning U.S. export licensing policy more closely with that of other COCOM members, the executive's institutions continued to pursue a policy at odds with U.S. allies and the wishes of American business by regulating many commodities not directly related to military application and by subjecting American exporters to lengthy license processing.

The executive's perspective on COCOM versus that of Congress and the ideological and operational disparities between the United States and the other COCOM nations are complex matters. The United States has negotiated with its European allies to control exports through a multilateral export control mechanism—the Coordinating Committee or COCOM—since 1949. Many commodities are currently subject to review by COCOM, as well as by domestic agencies. COCOM's list of products for review consists of many items on the Department of Commerce's commodity control list, in addition to arms, ammunition, and atomic energy materials. The COCOM list is not made public so as not to highlight the areas in which the West maintains a technological lead over communist countries. Three categories are noted on the COCOM list: items on List I are subject to complete embargo; items on List II are subject to quantitative restrictions; and items on List III are embargoed at the discretion of the individual nation. The criteria for determining whether an item should be included on any list and its subsequent allocation to a particular list include consideration of the type of technology to be transferred and the availability of alternative sources of supply.

Each COCOM nation organizes its own system of controls, using export licensing as the basic instrument. A voting rule of unanimity governs the collective decisions of COCOM. Each member may control additional items unilaterally. In fact, the U.S. government has always controlled a wide range of products not controlled by its COCOM partners. Although the COCOM list is intended to be an embargo list, exceptions may be made for individual cases approved for export under the export control procedures of the originating member country. The exporting member nation must present a request for an exception through its delegate to COCOM. Requests for exceptions are also subject to the unanimity rule, and a proposed export may take place only if all members agree that it does not constitute a security risk. Historically, the COCOM list was revised every three years and exception requests reviewed weekly.

Because of the differing viewpoints between the United States and its COCOM allies on export controls and because by 1970 the United States was no longer the sole or even principal source of high technology, the COCOM consensus weakened, and a greater commercial rivalry among members arose. Although a general agreement about the need to maintain a military embargo against the Soviet bloc for reasons of Western security remained intact, the COCOM allies did not share a consensus for broader economic or industrial warfare against the Eastern bloc. Responding to this situation, Congress mandated in the 1969 act that U.S. licensing procedures become attuned to the changing economic and political balance between the United States and its COCOM allies. However, as discussed, the executive made clear its opposition to this recommendation in its testimony before the House and Senate.

Despite Congress's urgings, the United States continued to pursue a more generally restrictive policy. The United States continued to control a large number of product categories not controlled by our COCOM allies. In 1972, the United States maintained unilateral controls on 461 classifications of goods and technology not under multilateral control.[65] The U.S. Commodity Control List as of September 1978 still contained, by one estimate, 207 entries of which 123 were COCOM controlled and 84 were unilaterally controlled by the United States.[66] By another government estimate, the United States unilaterally controlled 38 unique industrial item categories in 1979.[67] Bertsch's study summarized the U.S. position during the decade:

> Although supporting much East-West trade liberalization, the United States reacted negatively to most efforts to loosen the strategic COCOM embargo in the 1970s. The United States continued, for example, to utilize its veto to avoid decontrols involving deletions from and exceptions to the embargo list.[68]

Although the United States and other COCOM countries mutually agreed to one set of lists of controlled products and technologies, disparities in outlook and policies manifested themselves through differing national interpretations of both the list and enforcement policies.⁶⁹ Requests for exceptions to COCOM controls were also problematic.⁷⁰

The divergence was not solely the result of ideological or technological differences. Institutional processes also prevented U.S. licensing practices from aligning with those of COCOM. The process by which the United States arrived at its position for COCOM's list review in the 1970s continued to involve complex, time-consuming interagency coordination within the U.S. bureaucracy.

In addition to the Advisory Committee on Export Policy (ACEP), the interdepartmental committee which coordinates unilateral U.S. export control policy, a second interdepartmental group, the Economic Defense Advisory Committee (EDAC), chaired by the State Department,⁷¹ coordinates U.S. participation in multilateral policy through COCOM. The EDAC also decides whether COCOM exception requests to export controlled items should be approved. The EDAC operates under a rule of unanimity as well.

The EDAC's slowness in ruling on licensing and exception requests and business's lack of access to the process of administrative policy formulation as it applies to COCOM contributed to slow licensing. For example, in data submitted to the House of Representatives one company demonstrated that over a two-year period the processing time for over 100 of its USSR/East European license applications for COCOM-controlled products was more than $6\frac{1}{2}$ months.⁷² Similarly, a draft report of the President's Task Force to Improve Export Administration Licensing Procedures noted that in 1976 the necessity to obtain COCOM approval added an average of 40 days to the processing time of most U.S. export cases.⁷³ These delays occurred despite a 1974 requirement that license applications be approved or disapproved within 90 days.

The U.S. business community asserted that the more complex and time-consuming U.S. COCOM licensing process was a competitive detriment not faced to the same degree by businesses located in other COCOM member nations. Several industries alleged specifically that processing time is longer in the United States than abroad and that other COCOM countries provide advantages to their exporters by giving them a better idea of which applications will receive favorable action; they refer applications for COCOM exceptions with less preliminary screening and require from the exporter less documentation with regard to the item or proof that the item will not be diverted for strategic uses.⁷⁴

United States industries also expressed the desire to participate more actively in COCOM policy formulation, as it believed European businesses often did:

> We have observed that, in the computer field at least, the U.S. COCOM delegate in Paris is given technological support by a representative of a nonprofit organization under contract to the Department of Defense. In the same COCOM negotiations, the British delegate has the direct support of the British computer firm, International Computers, Ltd. (ICL), which enjoys ten percent British government ownership, and the French delegate is directly supported by a representative of the subsidized French computer firm known as CII (Compagnie International pour l'Informatique).[75]

Ironically, the insularity of the American executive from the business community, which often is considered evidence of weakness vis-à-vis its society, is in this instance a source of independent authority for the executive and its institutions in formulating export control policy.

■ Conclusion

Most political and legal scholarship has underestimated the executive's role in U.S. trade policy. In practice, the executive has garnered much power and influence over export regulation, as demonstrated in the legislating and implementing of export control policy.

During passage of the 1969 Export Administration Act the executive defined a policy position distinct from that of the congressional majority, a position that emphasized the executive's right to define the nation's security and foreign policy interests and to use export controls to serve these interests. The executive was more cohesive than Congress and better able to maintain its position over the course of the legislative process. The executive also possessed considerable leverage over Congress because of its expertise. Congress ultimately would defer to the executive's ability to make control list determinations and assess the foreign availability of controlled products. Finally, the executive's traditional role in defining U.S. security interests contributed to its ability to blunt certain congressional reforms. For example, Congress retracted its plan to create judicial oversight for the actions of executive institutions in recognition of the political (if not constitutional) challenge to the executive this reform represented.

In export control policy execution, the executive has had a great deal of authority delegated to it under the statutes discussed,[76] and it has used this authority to foster institutional capabilities and to pursue priorities which often differed from the congressional priorities of export expansion, improved responsiveness to the exporting community, and policy harmonization with COCOM members. Moreover, the executive's isolation from the business community —often perceived as a sign of weakness, lack of control, or lack of coordinating authority—is, in this area, a source of strength, permitting greater flexibility in pursuit of an autonomous export control policy.

In sum, institutional arrangements, capabilities, history, and policy orientation interacted to influence policy outcomes, resulting in policies different from congressional directives or the desires of the American exporting community. Institutions were slow to change during the 1970s and, lacking sustained pressure from within the executive to liberalize policy, pursued a conservative policy more in keeping with that of the 1950s and 1960s.

4. INSTITUTIONAL INFLUENCE ON LICENSING: THE REFORMS OF 1974, 1977, AND 1979

THE 1974, 1977, and 1979 reforms of the Export Administration Act occurred in the waning years of détente. The enthusiasm that accompanied the signing of SALT I and the enormous Soviet grain purchase of 1972 had passed. Congress, with the passage of the Jackson-Vanik amendment, defeated Most Favored Nation treatment for the Soviet Union which had been embodied in the 1972 U.S.-Soviet trade agreement; by 1974, the public had concluded that the sale of grain to the Soviets contributed to inflation in domestic food prices.[1]

Nonetheless, during the mid-1970s both houses of Congress still wished to facilitate the growth of American exports, including East-West trade, as long as this goal did not endanger national security. Consequently, the primary purpose of amendments during this period was to improve the licensing process by clarifying and making more consistent the policies and procedures of the 1969 Export Administration Act.

The Carter administration generally approved of congressional efforts to expand East-West trade and, at least in the early years of the administration, did not seek to politicize trade issues overtly. As late as September 1978, the President announced a national export policy which raised expectations that the executive would take meaningful steps to create trade incentives. He added:

> Equally important will be the reduction of Government-imposed disincentives and barriers which unnecessarily inhibit our firms from selling abroad. We can and will continue to administer the laws and policies affecting the international business community firmly and fairly, but we can also dis-

charge that responsibility with a greater sensitivity to the importance of exports than has been the case in the past.[2]

Yet, by 1978, President Carter, in response to the Soviet Union's treatment of American journalists and of Soviet dissidents Anatoly Scharansky and Aleksandr Ginzburg, imposed controls on petroleum equipment exports to the Soviet Union and reversed an earlier position by denying a pending application for the export of a computer to TASS, the official news agency of the Soviet Union. Both policies were implemented under the executive's foreign policy export control authority under the Export Administration Act. The Soviet invasion of Afghanistan in 1979 hastened the trend toward a harder line on East-West trade.

License processing and institutional operations, however, remained relatively consistent despite the ebb and flow of U.S.-Soviet relations and the dramatic use of foreign policy controls. This chapter will focus on the effects of executive institutions in shaping policy through day-to-day processing of license applications in the mid to late 1970s.

Congress attempted to expedite license processing in 1974, 1977, and 1979. It viewed license processing delays as a serious impediment to the more liberal export control policy it enunciated in the 1969 act. The executive institutions involved, while expressing their concern over continued delays, opposed any and all fundamental reforms in their licensing procedures. In practice, delays persisted and institutional procedures and performance remained fundamentally unchanged. This chapter documents the autonomy of executive institutions in license processing, identifies the factors which contributed to unabated institutional delays, and discusses the bureaucracy's resistance to change.

■ The Export Administration Act Amendments

In response to chronic licensing delays, in 1974 and 1977, Congress made significant amendments to the Export Administration Act in an effort to clarify, simplify, and thereby expedite the interagency export licensing process. In 1974, Congress required that license applications be approved or disapproved within 90 days, except in unusual circumstances which were meaningfully explained to the applicant.

By 1977, however, Congress recognized that "because applications still languish in the bureaucracy, unaccounted for, for months," a stronger congressional directive was needed. Despite the 1974 amendment, licensing delays continued:

> For example, a study conducted by a Presidential task force showed the following: (1) A random sample of 34 relatively simple applications which did not have to be referred to the formal interagency review process took an average of 93 days to decide; (2) a random sample of computer applications referred to the Department of Defense under section 4(h) of the act took an average of four months to decide; and (3) in 1975, 1,105 applications, which included nearly 20 percent of the Communist-destination applications, took more than the statutory 90 days to decide and 18 took over a year. Typically, objections to an export license application are raised in the confines of the bureaucracy; the applicant is neither meaningfully informed of the causes of the delay nor given a chance to respond.[3]

A separate study conducted by the U.S. Congress Office of Technology Assessment reported the following numbers of license applications pending for more than 90 days:[4]

Period Ending	Applications
1975	1,105
1976	689
1977	1,032

Consequently, the 1977 amendments set stricter standards for processing license applications.[5]

Finally, in response to continuing criticism of delays and in recognition that they usually involved those applications requiring interagency review, a reform act in 1979 provided that the Secretary of Commerce must complete an initial screening and notify the applicant within ten days of the application's sufficiency and any need for interagency or COCOM review. Further, the 1979 act limited the time for review by the consulted agency and permitted the applicant to petition the Secretary of Commerce, or, ultimately, a federal district court if the Secretary failed to respond to its petition.[6]

Before considering agency compliance with the new congressional guidelines, it is important to note the practical and policy importance of licensing delays.[7] According to the American exporting community, the direct results of delays include exports lost or business inhibited from attempting to export. Related practical effects include increased business costs, lost jobs, a damaged reputation for American business as a reliable supplier of goods, and, ironically, a reduction in technological preeminence to the extent that U.S. technology is protected from the stimulus of market forces. From a policy standpoint, the effect is a more restrictive export control program than that envisioned by Congress or American business.[8]

Exporters further maintain that the effect of U.S. licensing procedures as a disincentive to U.S. exports has been hidden by the relatively small percentage of export license applications actually denied. In 1977, Congress, in a written interrogatory to representatives of American industry, expressed the notion this way:

> Could you explain how the current law, which results in less than one-half of one percent (approximately 325 out of 65,000) of the licenses for export being denied, is a negative law, inhibiting exports?[9]

A coalition of domestic industries responded:

> The actual denial of export licenses does not have a major effect upon exports. The licensing system—its complexity, its arbitrariness, its lengthy bureaucratic procedures, its overlapping and multiple jurisdiction—has an inhibiting effect upon exporters.[10]

Responding to the same question by Congress, James Gray, President, National Machine Tool Builders' Association, noted that, although on the surface the statistic of 365 denials out of 65,000 applications seems insignificant, three very important factors must be kept in mind. First, an application denial rate of less than 0.6 percent fails to reflect the impact of those denials in economic terms. For example, the denial of a single machine tool export license could result in the loss not only of the specific order but, perhaps more important, of millions of dollars in follow-up business for a U.S. manufacturer. On the national level such a loss would further contribute to the worsening of the U.S. trade deficit. Second, the application denial rate fails to measure the number of U.S. manufacturers who simply stop applying for licenses because of frustrating past experiences. Third, the basic problem faced by machine tool builders is license delays rather than outright denials. Excessive delays in many cases amount to denials because contracts are cancelled during the lengthy processing of the license. Once this cancellation occurs, the foreign customer simply does not ask the U.S. exporter to bid on future contracts. Purchasers eventually look to other Western countries to supply their needs or develop the necessary technology themselves.[11]

The importance of licensing delays was a theme echoed by an independent governmental analysis of the export control apparatus. In summarizing the findings, J. Kenneth Fasick, Director, International Division, U.S. General Accounting Office, alleged that the complex regulatory system makes it difficult for exporters to know how and why the government makes its decisions. He added that this uncertainty hinders business operations and is inconsistent with Congress's trade expansion goals. Furthermore, he suggested that it is quite possible that many businesses simply ignore the idea of exporting because of the uncertainty and frustration the system creates.

Fasick described the real effects of licensing delay as follows:

> As shown in our October 1978 report, the delays in approving licenses have been an increasing problem. Since exporters have important deadlines they must meet in order to preserve long term international trading relationships, the delays and uncertainty in obtaining export licensing decisions damages their reputation as suppliers and further business can be lost. Thus the real impact on U.S. exporters is probably greater than the fact of a few denials.[12]

The heads of the executive institutions charged with processing licenses, however, consistently lobbied against stricter deadlines on the grounds that agency discretion and thoughtful review were required in licensing decisions to protect national security, that they were already sufficiently responsive and open to the export sector, and that they were making every effort to process applications more efficiently.[13]

For example, in 1979, business interests supported a congressional initiative that would provide clear and mandatory deadlines or "suspense points," at which time an agency was bound to render a decision on an application. In addition, congressional oversight was thought to be necessary to ensure that the deadlines were not used by the bureaucracy to deny licenses on the ground of lack of time for their full consideration.[14]

The Commerce Department, while voicing sympathy for business frustration, opposed mandatory deadlines as impractical:

> Those of us responsible for administering the export control system are aware of the hardships imposed on exporters by virtue of the time it sometimes takes to approve an export license. While we are strongly in favor of measures which will expedite case flow, we do not believe the system will benefit by writing rigid deadlines and automatic escalation provisions into the law. They simply do not work as a practical matter.[15]

Commerce attributed the primary source of licensing delays to the need to conduct in-depth technical analyses and make complex policy judgments within the bureaucracy on a large and increasing number of applications.[16] Long processing time was also, according to government spokesmen, the product of serious substantive disagreement over policy and technical issues, rather than simple bureaucratic delay. Consequently, the administering agencies repeatedly threatened that mandatory decision dates would merely increase the number of license application denials. The Commerce Department explained that it would be compelled to deny a pending application when facing a mandatory licensing deadline.

The department suggested instead that, for reasons of policy flexibility and national security, internal departmental guidelines would best address the issue of time limits. It proposed an internal agency system that would establish fixed numbers of days for each stage of licensing and would simplify the process involved. The Commerce Department made clear that its proposal differed from Congress's proposal in that at no stage in the process would it require that a definite decision be made on the case.[17] The Commerce Department ultimately prevailed as Congress removed suspense points from the 1979 act, thus revealing one instance where the variety of policy instruments, prerogatives (especially exemption from judicial review), and expertise acquired by the administering agencies over the years was used as leverage in influencing the course of congressional reforms.

■ Institutional Implementation of the Amendments

The business community's complaints over licensing delays were justifiable. Delays persisted despite the congressional intentions expressed in the 1974, 1977, and 1979 reforms. Although the 1974 amendments set a 90-day limit on the entire licensing process, the number of license applications pending for more than 90 days in 1978 totaled almost 2,000 applications—nearly twice the 1977 figure.[18]

In addition, private studies suggest with regard to many high-technology industries that delays actually increased after the 1977 reforms. For example, Hewlett-Packard Corporation documented that despite the processing requirements written into the 1974 and 1977 amendments, licensing delays were "just as bad as ever."[19] Hewlett-Packard studied 1,900 of its applications for COCOM-controlled goods to be exported to East European and Soviet destinations from 1971 to 1978. The results of this survey demonstrated that, except for a slight improvement in 1977, the amount of time required to reach a licensing decision in 1978 was almost identical to the period 1971–76.[20]

Moreover, this pattern of delay persisted into the 1980s. For example, 18 months after passage of the 1979 act, Paul T. O'Day, Acting Under Secretary for International Trade, Department of Commerce, confessed:

> Mr. Chairman, I wish that I could report that we are well within the statutory guidelines on all our cases, but that is not so. At the beginning of [April 1981], the Office of Export Administration had 4,567 cases in process. Of this total, 1,610 had been in process over 30 days, 1,013 over 90 days, and 668 over 180 days.[21]

Under Secretary for Trade Administration Lionel Olmer testified that in fiscal year 1982, 1,530 licenses took between 90 and 179 days to process, and 350 took more than 180 days.[22]

Rarely of direct concern to important executive actors, licensing delays were in large measure attributable to the complex multi-agency license application review process. Occasionally, licensing delays were purposeful. Executive institutions used delays to forestall either the approval or denial of a license application.[23] Delays of this sort, however, were not the norm. Institutional factors were a more significant cause. Especially in the area of high-technology exports, licensing was an increasingly segmented process subject to the scrutiny of several agencies. In general the Department of Defense examined license applications from a broad-gauge national security standpoint.[24] The Department of State, responsible for reviewing export controls imposed for foreign policy purposes and for chairing COCOM multilateral reviews, viewed export licensing from a diplomatic standpoint.[25] The Commerce Department—as a result of the disparate views of the agencies it must consult, and the ambivalent act which controls exports while it simultaneously recognizes the need to stimulate American export performance—failed to adopt clear policy guidelines and continued to frustrate many segments of the American business community.[26] Furthermore, the Commerce Department's export control function places it at odds with its traditional constituency, the American business community, and thus undermines its authority as an interagency player.

Without exaggerating the importance of interagency disputes or presuming that interagency disputes were a consistent feature of U.S. export control policy that frustrated congressional reforms, evidence suggests that by the late 1970s, differing agency viewpoints contributed to delays and hence to a more restrictive policy.[27] The Departments of State, Defense, and Commerce performed different functions in the formulation of policy and brought different viewpoints to their respective roles.

In addition, the original decision-making process based on precedent remained fundamentally unchanged throughout the 1970s and contributed to the system's slowness and its resistance to reform. As noted in David Baldwin's study, the institutional determination of what constitutes a strategic good has not changed in over forty years:

> The one-case-at-a-time approach based on scrutinizing a given item in order to determine its intrinsic military significance still seems to be firmly ensconced in the policy-making process . . . the basic analytic principles applicable to determining the strategic qualities of a given technology are really the same. . . .[28]

In addition to the analytical problems associated with the case-by-case method,[29] its ad hoc nature contributed to a lack of clear or uniform guidelines and to delays.

In a 1976 "Report to the Congress" on East-West trade problems, the General Accounting Office (GAO) reached precisely these conclusions. The report explained how the disparate policy positions adopted by the various departments involved in export control resulted in a lack of interagency agreement on criteria for controls and on whether foreign policy, commercial, or defense considerations should dominate policy on trade with Communist states. Executive branch agencies, the report added, differed regarding licensing standards and procedures to be followed in administering controls.[30] The report described the gradations within and between agencies:

> Defense's Office of Strategic Trade wants a voice in every control decision. Defense is reluctant to relinquish or delegate any authority to Commerce's Office of Export Administration because it believes that office does not have the technical capability to insure that licensing restrictions are properly applied. Commerce has conflicting priorities and coordination problems. Its Bureau of East-West Trade cooperates closely with State in promoting trade with Communist countries, but OEA, part of the Bureau, shares many of the concerns of Defense and has coordination problems with Commerce's Office of International Marketing. State's export officials in the field have different perceptions than those in Washington concerning the effectiveness and importance of export controls, cooperation of COCOM countries in adhering to multilateral controls, and the effect of various COCOM country practices on foreign business competition.[31]

J. Kenneth Fasick, Director of the International Division of the GAO, further concluded that because of an "absence of agreement on criteria and standards for determining which goods should be controlled and whether foreign policy, commercial or defense considerations should dominate export control policy," licensing procedures were unduly slow and awkward.[32]

A second study of export licensing procedures conducted during 1978 reached similar conclusions. At the request of President Carter, the National Governors Association established a standing Committee on International Trade and Foreign Relations in conjunction with the Rusk Center at the University of Georgia. Its mandate was to analyze the implementation of the Export Administration Act and to recommend changes in the coming congressional session. The report, as summarized by the committee's co-chair, Fredrick W. Huszagh, noted four basic characteristics of the export licensing process: (1) a multiplicity of bureaucratic agencies involved in the licensing process (six or more for high-technology licensing requests) that bring independent and differing viewpoints on the purposes to be served by export controls; (2) a lack of agreement on a hierarchy of goals, most notably whether trade or security considerations should predominate; (3) a recognition of the need to respond to licensing deadlines; and (4) a diffusion of authority which shifts responsibility for managing applications within and between agencies, resulting in great uncertainty for exporters.[33] As was discussed in chapter 1, these characteristics can be traced to original institutional implementation of the 1949 Export Control Act.

The Rusk Center study, based on 50 in-depth interviews which systematically surveyed the attitudes of individuals within the relevant agencies, revealed that the executive branch presented a significant barrier to congressional reform. The executive agencies preferred to implement the act as they always had and were reluctant to permit Congress to fetter their discretion in implementing policy. Furthermore, the failure of past congressional statutory efforts to translate into corresponding policy reforms was attributed, in large measure, to the independent, intervening role of bureaucratic institutions.[34]

The business community, an admittedly interested group, also believed that the contentious nature of U.S. export control policy could be traced to embedded bureaucratic practices coupled with the executive's ambivalence about relinquishing its discretion in implementing controls for foreign policy and national security purposes. The business community noted that institutional structure had led historically to an interagency decision-making process at odds with the congressionally espoused goal of expanding American exports. In a discussion paper submitted to the Congress during its 1979 hearings, John A. Chambers, Vice President, Satra Corporation (an international trading company), offered this summary:

> Relegating one's self to the specific issue at hand, *i.e.*, the Export Administration Act of 1969, one must first acknowledge that it was initially implemented with a "negative" attitude in the bureaucracy. Since the Congress passed the basic legislation, there has been a continuous struggle with the former implementers of the negative Export Control Act of 1949, who

are now the managers of the positive Export Administration Act of 1969.[35]

Chambers placed the responsibility for bureaucratic intransigence squarely on the lack of clear guidelines from the President and the disparate views of the administering agencies.[36]

■ Conclusion

In view of the pattern of repeatedly unsuccessful efforts to institute meaningful institutional reforms, it is fair to ask whether, in this area, Congress or, more accurately, those members of Congress interested in export control policy were sincere in their efforts to make the system swifter, more equitable, and more accountable through amending legislation. In his seminal work *The End of Liberalism*, Theodore Lowi identified a general tendency of Congress to delegate responsibility and authority to the executive. Is Lowi's observation relevant to export reforms directed at license processing? Was reform legislation a half-hearted effort to appease business interests without creating clear, enforceable standards for the bureaucracy to follow, and thus were consequent policies not a victory for the executive or an example of institutional autonomy but merely evidence of an earlier forfeiture of control by Congress?

Though no one could claim to have an accurate barometer of the sincerity of Congress or particular members of that body, the phenomenon identified by Lowi does not appear wholly relevant to congressional-executive relations in export control lawmaking. Discussions with current and past members of the executive and legislative branches confirm that Congress was genuine or perceived as genuine by members of the executive branch and was frustrated by its inability to fashion effective licensing deadlines and more efficient licensing practices. The explanation for Congress's repeated attempts and repeated failure to make the system work better and faster and its acquiescence to the executive's claimed needs for flexibility were more often attributed not to insincerity, lack of interest, or carte blanche delegation, but to Congress's inability to instill good management through legislation or oversight.[37] To use a 1980s term, Congress was attempting to "micromanage," and manage well, an entrenched, diffused, inefficient, and generally unaccountable bureaucracy making several thousand highly technical decisions a year. Such efforts were bound to fail in view of the executive's well-established institutional capabilities and control over export licensing.

The complexity of the licensing process and the case-by-case method of reaching licensing decisions inhibited Congress's ability to define the executive's authority or shape the system's operations. The case-by-case system, which requires multiple independent decisions on each good or technology to be exported, is not manageable by rigid deadlines. Congress recognized that in the event an agency felt it could not reach a decision by an impending deadline, it would choose to deny a license—a result at odds with the congressional goal. Congress also fundamentally believed in the necessity of export controls and reluctantly realized that the rate of processing individual case decisions would necessarily remain a matter of some executive discretion. Consequently, Congress repeatedly resorted to efforts to reform procedures and attempts to guide or exhort the executive toward greater efficiency and openness rather than eliminating aspects of executive authority or limiting discretion through the setting of rigid deadlines.

What is apparent in this study of license processing reform attempted by the 1974 and 1977 amendments and the 1979 act is the wide gap between congressional aspirations and reality. The continuing delays were, in part, caused by the multiplicity of consulted agencies, but delays were not merely a function of the number of agencies involved. Delays were also a consequence of the method of agency decision-making, the differing, endogenously defined orientations of these administering agencies (traceable in some agencies to the bureaucracy's initial mandate), the occasional purposeful disobedience of administrative agencies, and the slowness with which these agencies responded to societal, i.e., congressional, pressures for change.

Export license processing was consistently at odds with congressional and interest group demands. Executive institutions shaped policy to fit institutionally defined goals and methods. Institutions only occasionally opposed the will of Congress by purposeful delays. More often, however, institutions, in pursuit of established duties and obligations, continued procedures certain to impede efforts to expedite license processing. The explanation for the slowness of institutional reform may lie in part with institutional history. For example, the diffusion of licensing decisions and the consequent vesting of institutions' interests in the process foreclosed the possibility of a more expeditious system of processing through centralized decision-making or a Commerce Department override.

In addition, executive institutions administered by appointees and permanent bureaucrats were insulated in some measure from societal pressures for change. Finally, it appears that part of the explanation lies in the fact that legislation is an inadequate means of holding accountable entrenched executive institutions or changing institutional practices.

5. EXECUTIVE AUTONOMY AND FOREIGN POLICY EXPORT CONTROLS

THE executive, at times, has articulated and pursued successfully a discernibly different export control policy from that of Congress or domestic interest groups. Chapter 3 mentioned briefly the influence and importance of the President and the inner circle of presidential advisors and cabinet heads within the executive with regard to export liberalization during the early 1970s. The relative autonomy of the President and highly placed officials within the executive branch is most clearly evident in the executive's increasing use of export controls for foreign policy purposes in the late 1970s.

The furtherance of U.S. foreign policy interests, as distinct from the protection of national security, was a statutorily recognized purpose of the 1949 Export Control Act and later the 1969 Export Administration Act. The 1969 act, like its predecessor, authorized the President to regulate the export of goods and technology "to the extent necessary to further significantly the foreign policy of the United States and to fulfill its international responsibilities."[1] Nonetheless, until the late 1970s, explicit foreign policy export controls were peripheral to the export control system.

For more than thirty years, the export controls governing East-West trade—despite the breadth of products and technologies encompassed—were defined as controls serving national security rather than foreign policy purposes. Although foreign policy considerations motivated the continuation of a limited number of export controls initially promulgated for national security purposes,[2] earlier uses of export controls for avowed foreign policy purposes were confined to two policies during the mid-1970s which involved significant multilateral cooperation; the short-lived embargo on trade with Southern Rhodesia and the ban on arms exports to

South Africa.[3] These policies were instituted pursuant to U.S. international obligations under the United Nations Charter.[4]

In 1977 and 1978, however, the executive's explicit use of export controls for a variety of foreign policy purposes became commonplace, and the extent of foreign policy controls in terms of country and product coverage became significant. Before passage of the 1979 act, the Carter administration issued four sets of foreign policy controls: (1) the prohibition of all exports to the military and police forces of South Africa and Namibia;[5] (2) the controls on exports to the Soviet Union of products and technology related to oil and gas exploration and production;[6] (3) the statutory prohibition of exports (except agricultural products) to Uganda;[7] and (4) the prohibition of exports of crime control and detection equipment and related technical data, without a validated license, to any destination except a NATO country, Japan, Australia, or New Zealand.[8]

Highly placed policymakers within the executive initiated two of the foreign policy export controls: the prohibition against exports to the South African and Namibian police and controls on the export of oil and gas equipment to the Soviet Union. In fact, President Carter personally decided to limit the export of petroleum equipment to the Soviet Union.[9] Both policies stemmed from the Carter administration's emphasis on human rights.[10] The controls directed against Uganda, however, were initiated by Congress, and the expanded limitations on the export of crime control technology evolved from executive-congressional interaction.

The executive's authority to undertake foreign policy export controls was virtually unbridled during the 1970s. Before 1979, the executive's authority to use export controls for foreign policy purposes was broader and less well-defined than its national security authority. In the 1969 act, Congress differentiated foreign policy controls from "national security controls," i.e., those controls intended to restrict exports that would make "a significant contribution to the military potential of any other nation or nations which would prove detrimental to the national security of the United States."[11] Because shipments of purely military goods and technologies were regulated under a separate statute,[12] the President's national security control authority was limited to regulating "dual-use" items of both civilian and potential military applicability; prohibiting in most instances their export directly or indirectly to Communist countries. However, export controls invoked for foreign policy purposes could be extended to all goods, strategic and nonstrategic. Foreign policy controls, unlike national security controls, had no mechanism such as COCOM to coordinate their restrictions with the practices of U.S. allies. Because allied nations were less likely to cooperate with export restraints not directly linked to their security interests, foreign policy controls also became a source of policy divergence between the United States and its allies.[13]

Furthermore, while the Export Administration Act of 1969, as amended, stated that the executive should consider the foreign availability of comparable products before applying national security controls, it was mute with regard to the executive's necessary considerations before imposing foreign policy controls. In a situation where comparable goods were available outside the United States, a purchaser could simply shift to a supplier of comparable products in another country, thereby subverting the effectiveness of unilateral U.S. controls. Finally, the 1969 act also required semi-annual reports on foreign policy export controls, but these reports, by most estimations, did not adequately inform Congress or the public.[14]

The foreign policy export controls of the late 1970s and the recognition of the executive's virtually limitless discretion spurred legislation amending the relevant section of the Export Administration Act in 1979. Passage of the 1979 act marked Congress's first attempt to limit presidential authority to control exports for foreign policy purposes. This chapter will demonstrate that during passage of the act the executive was often successful in opposing and weakening congressional amendments which would have restrained executive flexibility in using foreign policy export controls. Moreover, despite Congress's clear intent to limit such use to a "last resort" after full consideration of the costs and alternatives, and despite new administrative burdens on the executive, including a variety of reporting and consulting requirements, the executive freely and forcefully pursued foreign policy export controls without restraint from and in disregard of both the letter and spirit of the new law.

■ The Export Administration Act of 1979

The Export Administration Act of 1979 continued the basic purpose and operating principles of its predecessor.[15] Its major reforms were directed at increasing the role of Congress in evaluating the exercise of foreign policy controls by the President, making domestic and international licensing review procedures more efficient and open, and clarifying the role of the Defense and Commerce departments in establishing the lists of "militarily critical technologies" and controlled commodities.[16]

Although not as contentious as passage of the 1969 act which preceded it or the 1985 act which followed, the legislative debate surrounding the 1979 act lasted several months and ranged from matters of national security to the export of domestic cattle hides. Congressional debate on the bill centered on the Commerce Department's role as administrator of national security export controls and the completion of a list of critical military technologies designed to identify vital, keystone technologies. The final version of the bill gave the Defense Department primary responsibility for compiling the list of critical technologies and maintained the joint role of the Commerce and Defense departments in deciding which items should be added to the list of controlled commodities.

Both the Senate bill, S. 737, and the House bill, H.R. 4034, established criteria for the President to consider before imposing foreign policy controls. The House bill gave Congress 60 days to veto a proposed foreign policy export control. The Senate bill required only that the President inform Congress within 30 days of his decision to impose such controls.

Both houses of Congress concluded that uncertainty over U.S. policy in this area had discouraged potential exports and tarnished the reputation of U.S. exporters as reliable suppliers. Thus, in the estimation of Congress, legislation was necessary to foster consistency in policy and closer cooperation with America's allies.[17] Congress also noted that controls applied for foreign policy reasons often restricted the export of goods and technology freely available from foreign suppliers, often from America's allies. Yet, Congress found no evidence that the effects of such controls received due consideration or that efforts were made to obtain agreement by our allies to adopt similar restrictions on their exports.[18] Congress thus urged greater consideration of foreign availability of goods controlled for foreign policy reasons.

Foreign policy export controls were used with increasing frequency in the late 1970s and came under increasing attack from the business community, academia, and America's allies. The business community believed that, without serving national security interests, they abrogated existing contracts and foreclosed future ones, damaged the reputation of U.S. exporters, and exacerbated the ever worsening U.S. balance of trade.[19] Policy analysts criticized the controls as an ineffective means of achieving foreign policy objectives and concluded that these policies were costly and served little more than symbolic, signaling, or displacement functions.[20] Furthermore, because no means existed for coordinating unilateral U.S. foreign policy controls, they were a source of contention with allies who did not share foreign policy objectives or who disagreed over the use of export controls as the best means of achieving shared goals.[21]

As a result of these dissatisfactions, in the 1979 act Congress attempted to limit the situations where the President could use his foreign policy export control authority to those instances where the President had fully considered the likely effectiveness of the proposed controls in achieving their purpose, their compatibility with overall U.S. foreign policy, their effect on U.S. export performance generally and on the affected companies in particular, and the ability of the United States government to enforce them effectively in light of the foreign availability of the good or technology involved.[22] Congress also attempted to instill greater accountability of the President to Congress and the business community through consultation and reporting requirements. Congress required the President to find that: (1) the controls would be likely to change behavior in the target state; (2) the controls would not cause undue hardship to the U.S. economy or employment; and (3) successful negotiations with foreign governments eliminating the foreign availability of the controlled products were likely to occur.[23]

Congress gave serious consideration to the business community's criticism of the standard for assessing foreign availability in the proposed legislation. It noted that the standard in section 6(b) of the 1979 bill (the foreign policy section) was less stringent in its provisions regarding decontrol of a product when available from foreign sources than the standard in section 5 (the national security section), which required decontrol if foreign availability of a product existed unless the President reported to Congress the reasons for maintaining a control. Business representatives observed that "this lack of consistency between sections 5 and 6 forces us to hypothesize situations in which export license determinations would be styled as foreign policy decisions rather than matter[s] of military security as a means of denying a license in the face of foreign availability."[24] In view of the limited effectiveness and high cost of such controls, the business community recommended that "the same foreign availability restrictions be imposed on administrative authority for licensing controls based on foreign policy considerations as are imposed upon national security controls."[25]

The executive adopted a very different outlook. While espousing the need to expand exports, the executive opposed any changes in the 1979 bill that would effectively limit the executive's flexibility in imposing controls for foreign policy purposes, even in circumstances where the controls would not be effective in denying the country the goods or technology in question. In particular, the executive opposed the imposition of strict criteria that must be considered before imposing controls for foreign policy purposes.[26] In addition, the executive claimed that it already considered factors such as foreign availability in reaching its decisions, but that it was executive practice to impose controls regardless of its findings should it desire to do so for moral or symbolic reasons.[27]

The executive also opposed any provision permitting Congress to veto the imposition of foreign policy controls and rejected a requirement that the executive consult with affected industries or other governments *before* imposing foreign policy controls.[28] It characterized these restrictions as constitutional or practical encroachments on the President's ability to conduct foreign affairs.[29]

The provisions of the 1979 Export Administration Act on foreign policy export controls represented a compromise between the position of the executive and that of the business community on several issues and a capitulation by Congress to the executive's interest on several other issues. Nonetheless, the final legislation reflected the desire of many members of Congress to restrain the executive's use of foreign policy controls and limit executive discretion by various procedural and substantial provisions.

Congress made clear that the purpose of the 1979 act was to "emphasiz[e] the importance of exports to the United States economy and confin[e] the use of export controls to instances where controls are essential."[30] In addition to this and other hortatory provisions,[31] a variety of substantive limitations on the executive's foreign policy export control authority were written into the act, including: (1) a general limitation based on foreign availability; (2) a list of criteria for the President to consider before imposing foreign policy export controls; and (3) a provision that affected industries be consulted and Congress be notified before the imposition of foreign policy controls. Congress reserved veto authority over foreign policy controls encompassing agricultural products, but no other congressional veto provision was included in the 1979 act.

The foreign availability assessment provision was weak and its language porous. Section 4(c) of the 1979 act requires that the President not impose controls for foreign policy purposes on items available "without restriction" in significant quantities and comparable quality from foreign sources *unless* he finds adequate evidence that the absence of controls would prove detrimental to American foreign policy.[32] The Senate Banking Committee stated that this standard was not as strict as that required for national security controls:

> While the committee amendments require an assessment of foreign availability in both foreign policy and national security cases, the committee does not intend that the issue of foreign availability necessarily be given the same weight in both situations. Obviously, the usefulness of export controls in national security cases is substantially vitiated to the extent the country in question can obtain comparable goods or technologies from a country other than the United States. However, the committee agrees with the Administration position that there may be legitimate foreign policy reasons for denying exports to a particular country even if the only short-term trade effects might be to divert sales to our competitors.[33]

Similarly, with respect to foreign availability determinations, the committee made clear that the President was only required to determine whether foreign availability exists and attempt to eliminate it in appropriate situations. He was not precluded from using foreign policy export controls despite foreign availability:

> the bill *merely requires* the President to assess foreign availability and where it exists, determine whether he has adequate evidence that failing to control exports would be detrimental to U.S. foreign policy, and try to convince other exporting nations to join the United States in applying export controls. *The provision will not preclude the use of export controls for foreign policy purposes despite foreign availability.* [Emphasis added.][34]

It is impossible to credit the eventual weakening of the foreign availability provision in the 1979 act directly to the determined efforts of the executive to demonstrate to Congress that a binding criterion would unduly restrain the executive's flexibility in implementing foreign policy. Nonetheless, the Senate Banking Committee Report accompanying the 1979 act, in reaching the above findings, cited the State Department's warning that such a provision would hinder the executive's flexibility in responding to the "extreme acts" of other nations.[35] Ultimately, the committee chose to defer to the executive's expressed needs for maneuverability in the conduct of U.S. foreign affairs.

The 1979 act also attempted to provide detailed guidance on factors to be considered by the executive before implementing foreign policy controls, including: (1) the probability that the controls will achieve their intended purpose; (2) the compatibility of the controls with other U.S. foreign policy objectives; (3) the reaction of other countries; (4) the likely impact on the U.S. economy; (5) the ability of the United States to enforce the controls; and (6) the foreign policy consequences of not imposing the controls.[36] In legislating this provision, however, Congress, in response to executive demands for flexibility,[37] again emphasized the nonbinding nature of the factors. The committee report accompanying the legislation noted

> that the provision as amended would not preclude the President from reacting promptly to extreme situations, nor prevent him from imposing or maintaining export controls regardless of his conclusions with respect to the factors listed, nor require a public report if the President decided a public report was not in the national interest.[38]

The committee further noted that the new foreign policy provisions did not establish criteria to be met but rather set forth factors to be considered, and recognized that the President, having considered them, might find one or more irrelevant to a decision to impose or remove controls.[39]

The nonbinding nature of these factors is also reflected in the language of the statute which provides only that the President "shall consider" them before imposing export controls for foreign policy purposes. In addition, Congress required the President consult the business community and affected industries "as the Secretary [of Commerce] considers appropriate" before imposing controls and determine that reasonable efforts have been made to achieve their purpose through negotiation or alternative means.[40] Moreover, the President was required to consult with Congress "in every possible instance" before imposing a control and to report to

Congress regarding each of the specified factors he considered.[41] In addition to the obvious loopholes contained in these provisions, the 1979 act failed to define "consultation," did not require the executive to justify a failure to consult or report under the act, and did not provide for sanctions in cases of executive noncompliance.

The foreign policy "restraints" on the executive contained in the 1979 act were little more than procedural nuisances. The executive remained free to interpret if and when adherence to the provisions of the act was required. Sustained effort by the executive to retain flexibility over foreign policy controls, divisions within Congress over the degree to which it was willing to limit executive authority, and congressional deference to the executive's foreign affairs powers and prerogatives conspired to produce a tenuous and ambiguous act.

For example, the congressional language of the foreign policy provisions and the decision reached in conference to delete the House provision for a congressional veto reflected a willingness by Congress to accord the President some discretion in foreign affairs.[42] Those in Congress who favored a congressional veto, such as Jonathan B. Bingham (D-N.Y.), were unable to convince a majority of Senate conferees that a veto threat in the case of foreign policy controls was necessary to ensure advance notification by the executive to Congress.

Similarly, Congress was faced with business pressures to impose statutory limits on the executive's ability to use export controls to further foreign policy and in turn by objections from the administration that the section 6(b) provisions unduly restricted the President's ability to respond to crises. Congress chose language which it hoped would convey its intent that the executive refrain from using export controls as a means of achieving foreign policy objectives. Furthermore, Congress attempted to convey to the executive the message that it could not use foreign policy export controls until it had fully considered alternatives and the cost of controls and had consulted with Congress and affected industries.

The executive was a salient, generally unified participant in the lawmaking process. Congress, in contrast, while generally supportive of efforts to restrain the executive's foreign policy authority, often was divided over the best means to achieve this end. Congress also deferred to the executive's claimed need for flexibility, fearing undue restraint despite its dissatisfaction with the executive's use of foreign policy export controls. Congress preferred to guide the executive's use of controls rather than eliminate entirely the executive's authority. Nonetheless, Congress treated the foreign policy provisions seriously and expected the executive to do the same.[43]

■ Foreign Policy Export Controls in the 1980s

The second half of this chapter considers the capacity of the executive to exercise its foreign policy export control authority in view of the concerns voiced and restraints fashioned by Congress. In policy implementation, as well as in policy formulation, the President and his appointees pursued foreign policy controls in keeping with their independent understanding of their authority and with little regard for the congressional design. Despite congressional intentions, the 1979 reforms did not constrain the executive's use of export control policy for political purposes. Although section 6(b) of the act set forth specific factors for the President to consider when imposing, expanding, or extending foreign policy controls, the President was not bound to do more than consider the factors. In practice, the foreign policy prerogatives of the President have predominated over congressional wishes, expressed in the legislation, that considerations of domestic economic costs and the effectiveness of the controls be given greater weight and that the business community and Congress be fully and promptly informed.

Since the passage of the 1979 act a determined executive continued to curtail exports for foreign policy reasons in spite of the act. Most foreign policy controls in effect when the act was passed were extended by the executive, for example.[44] More important, new congressional guidelines did not curb efforts to limit exports to the Soviet Union following its invasion of Afghanistan. The foreign policy controls instituted by President Carter in this instance included the suspension of all validated export licenses for high-technology items destined for the Soviet Union; an embargo on grain shipments exceeding the limits provided for in a five-year U.S.-USSR agreement[45] (because this embargo involved an agricultural commodity, the control was also justified on national security grounds to avoid the possibility of a congressional veto); a ban on phosphate exports to the Soviet Union without a validated license and a strengthening of this control shortly thereafter to suspend all such exports;[46] a prohibition on all export transactions connected with the 1980 Summer Olympic Games in Moscow;[47] an extension of existing national security and foreign policy controls to Afghanistan that paralleled those imposed upon the Soviet Union;[48] and controls on certain exports to the Soviet Union's Kama River truck plant.[49]

In addition, the Carter administration employed a variety of economic sanctions, including an export embargo, against Iran. These controls were issued pursuant to the executive's emergency authority under the International Emergency Economic Powers Act.[50]

President Carter's foreign policy export control initiatives implemented under the Export Administration Act of 1979 received a mixed reception from Congress. Some controls, such as the Kama River controls and the Olympic boycott, were made with congressional support. The centerpiece of the administration's sanctions against the Soviet Union following the invasion of Afghanistan—the grain boycott—met with significant congressional opposition, however.

The Carter administration justified the grain boycott, instituted at the behest of the National Security Council and the Department of Defense, on both national security and foreign policy grounds to avoid the possible exercise of congressional veto power over controls on agricultural products imposed for foreign policy reasons. Under the sanctions, the United States limited its grain sales to the Soviet Union to 8 million metric tons in 1979 and rescinded its commitment to sell up to 25 million metric tons of grain in that year.

The grain embargo was sharply criticized during congressional hearings following its imposition, but the immediate congressional response did not extend to an attempt to use a legislative veto.[51] In general, Congress was reluctant to undermine the President's initiative or indirectly show approval of the Soviet Union's invasion of Afghanistan. However, many members of Congress were outspoken in their criticism of the efficacy of the sanction, their concern with minimizing the expected impact on U.S. farmers, and their disapproval of the administration's attempt to circumvent Congress by claiming the grain embargo to be both a national security and foreign policy export control.[52]

By late spring, congressional criticism of the grain embargo had increased.[53] Congressional opposition peaked in the summer of 1980 when members of Congress of both parties and in both houses introduced legislation to rescind the embargo. The House ultimately rejected an amendment to an appropriations bill prohibiting the Commerce Department from using funds to enforce the grain embargo, but the Senate approved the measure by voice vote. Following a pledge by President-elect Reagan to end the embargo, Congress deleted the amendment in conference.

Despite domestic and international opposition to the boycott, the Carter administration held firm and did not lift it, thus demonstrating the executive's endurance as well as initiative in the use of foreign policy export controls. In fact, although President Reagan lifted the embargo on April 24, 1981, the action was a more difficult and contentious decision for Ronald Reagan as President than it had been for Ronald Reagan as candidate.[54]

The Reagan administration changed the direction of U.S. export control policy, but it did not differ from the Carter Administration in either its willingness to use export controls for foreign policy purposes or its belief that, despite the 1979 act, the use and administration of export controls were the executive's prerogative. President Reagan declined to impose controls on East-West grain sales, but was more willing to restrict both U.S. and foreign companies from engaging in the sale of certain equipment and technology to the Soviet Union and its allies. Furthermore, while deemphasizing the use of foreign policy export controls for human rights purposes, the Reagan administration was committed to linking American export trade to its opposition to international terrorism and to using export controls as a means of expressing its dissatisfaction with the policies of other nations. In short, the presidential proclivity to use export controls for foreign policy purposes has proven to be decidedly bipartisan; changes in administration or in the substance of foreign policy have not reduced the executive's willingness to use foreign policy export controls despite the 1979 Export Administration Act.

President Reagan issued foreign policy export controls over oil and gas equipment and related technical data to the Soviet Union. These controls were imposed in two parts. The first part, imposed on December 30, 1981, expanded the existing requirement for validated export licenses for goods related to exploration and production to include those related to transmission and refinement. In addition, processing of all export licenses on goods destined for the Soviet Union was temporarily suspended. The second part of these controls, initiated in June 1982, expanded coverage of the oil and gas controls extraterritorially to include exports of foreign-origin goods and technical data by U.S.-owned or controlled companies abroad and foreign-produced products of U.S. technical data not previously subject to controls. These controls were imposed in response to the Soviet Union's "heavy and direct responsibility" for the repression in Poland. The officially stated purpose of the policy was to serve as a flexible tool to be used, when necessary and appropriate, to sensitize the Soviets to actions damaging to U.S. foreign policy interests.[55]

The pipeline controls were made at the urging of the National Security Council over significant domestic and international opposition and despite dissent within the administration from Secretary of State Alexander Haig and Secretary of Commerce Malcolm Baldrige. The extreme opposition, both domestic and international, to the second phase of the pipeline controls will be explored below. It is noteworthy, however, that phase one of the pipeline controls also received little public or congressional support. Even before implementation of the second phase of the controls, Representatives Paul Findley (R-Ill.) and Don Bonker (D-Wash.) introduced legislation to terminate them. Representative Findley, in a floor statement introducing the bill, said it "is clear that these sanctions do not work."[56]

Congressional dissatisfaction grew with the second phase of pipeline controls. After six months of controls, an increasing number of congressmen questioned their efficacy and noted the lack of allied support. Senator Charles Percy (R-Ill.), Chairman of the Senate Foreign Relations Committee, stated that the embargo had "no effect whatsoever on the Soviet Union."[57] Representative Robert Michel (R-Ill.) added, "We are aiming at the Soviet Union but we keep hitting the American worker . . . and we cannot persuade our allies to follow our lead."[58]

International opposition to the pipeline controls increased steadily after the first stage, and reached crisis proportions after imposition of phase two. In the interim between the first and second phases of the pipeline controls, the administration was warned by the international business and legal communities of potential political dangers and economic costs that could arise from extraterritorial application of the pipeline controls.[59] For example, a February 5, 1982 letter from Richard L. Lesher, President of the U.S. Chamber of Commerce, to President Reagan stated:

> We have been led to believe that the Administration is seriously considering sanctions against West European firms to force compliance with our foreign policy sanctions related to the Yamal pipeline. I want to share with you our concerns that reported U.S. actions under consideration would be unprece-

dented and may not be in the best interests of this country....
The possibility of extraterritorial controls over the activities of
West European firms utilizing U.S. technology raises serious
implications for U.S. foreign economic policy and our trade
relationships around the world.[60]

Moreover, the President and highest officers in the executive branch were aware that the Europeans opposed the first phase of the pipeline controls and would not tolerate any expansion of their extraterritorial reach.[61] Nonetheless, when the administration was unable to secure an agreement with the allies on the limitation of credit and credit terms to the Soviet Union during the Versailles summit, it extended the pipeline controls in unprecedented ways.[62]

The European reaction was sudden and angry. European governments with corporations under contract to supply commodities for the pipeline opposed the new controls in the press and in their formal public comments on the new regulations; they urged or required their companies to fulfill their contractual obligations in defiance of U.S. export control laws.[63] The European reaction was founded on both commercial and political considerations. European companies had signed contracts more than a year in advance of the controls. The contracts represented an important source of jobs and national income. One West German supplier, AG-Telefunken, claimed it could face bankruptcy without their pipeline contract worth $265 million.[64]

Perhaps more important to the Europeans than the immediate commercial costs were the political costs of acquiescing in a foreign policy that was not an indigenous European one. From the start, the Europeans did not attribute direct responsibility for the Polish situation to the Soviet Union. Instead, they favored a policy of maintaining the existing pattern of East-West cooperative arrangements as a means of eventually easing political tensions in Poland and encouraging a renewed dialogue between the Polish government, the Church, and Solidarity.[65] When the United States ordered the Europeans to adopt a policy of economic coercion toward the Soviet Union through the extraterritorial application of U.S. export control laws, the Europeans necessarily opposed the policy as an infringement on their commercial and political sovereignty.[66]

In the face of extreme opposition from Congress, the business community, and a unified coalition of the NATO allies, and under the urging of his Secretary of State, President Reagan reluctantly lifted the extraterritorial pipeline controls at the end of 1982.

The pipeline controls illustrate both the breadth and the limits on executive autonomy and discretion. First, the executive independently undertook this export control policy despite the strenuous opposition of the U.S. business community and America's allies.[67] It pursued the policy without the encouragement of the American public and Congress[68] to the point where the controls threatened permanent injury to the NATO alliance and may have exceeded the accepted jurisdictional bases of authority under international law. At that point, the executive retreated from the more extreme aspects of the controls,[69] yielding ultimately to combined domestic, international, and legal constraints.

President Reagan expanded existing foreign policy controls against Libya.[70] In an effort to "restrict a U.S. contribution to, and thereby to limit Libyan capacity to engage in activities detrimental to foreign policy of the United States," President Reagan twice extended the coverage of Libyan foreign policy controls under the Export Administration Act. On October 28, 1981, additional controls were imposed on small aircraft, helicopter, and other aircraft parts and avionics to "limit Libyan capacity to support military ventures in neighboring countries." Comprehensive export controls were imposed on March 12, 1982, requiring validated export licenses for all commodities and technical data, except food, agricultural, medical goods, and certain other items.[71] The policy guidelines enunciated in the regulations make clear that the purposes of the license requirements were to deny Libya U.S.-origin national security items, oil and gas equipment, and technical data unavailable from foreign sources and to monitor, but not necessarily deny, other exports.[72] The Reagan administration subsequently imposed additional sanctions against Libya under the International Emergency Economic Powers Act (IEEPA). The use of IEEPA, as opposed to the Export Administration Act, was in part an attempt by the executive to avoid an amendment to the foreign policy provisions of the Export Administration Act that prohibits breaking existing contracts through the use of nonemergency foreign policy export controls. The executive also employed the IEEPA in imposing foreign policy export controls against Nicaragua and extending economic sanctions directed at South Africa under the Export Administration Act. These policies will be discussed in chapter 6.

In continuing its use of foreign policy controls, the executive has largely ignored the guidelines set forth in the 1979 act. The Carter administration's reports to Congress regarding foreign availability assessment reveal that the executive was not dissuaded from imposing foreign policy export controls despite foreign availability of the controlled products, and did not feel compelled to explain meaningfully its decision to impose controls, despite foreign availability, to Congress. The 1980 report accompanying the Carter administration's extension of controls states that evidence "has been presented demonstrating that, notwithstanding foreign availability, the absence of these controls would prove detrimental to the foreign policy of the United States."[73] The evidence supplied by the report consisted of unsubstantiated conclusions reached by the Commerce Department.[74]

Similarly, the Reagan administration was chastised by its staunchest supporters in Congress for its "disappointing" assessment of foreign availability in extending foreign policy export controls. In a letter to Commerce Secretary Malcolm Baldrige, Senators Jake Garn (R-Utah) and John Heinz (R-Penn.) commented that the executive's February 26, 1982 report failed to comply with the 1979 Export Administration Act. Senators Garn and Heinz particularly criticized the report's cursory examination of foreign availability, stating that the foreign availability issue "is crucial and deserves more attention than that evidenced in the report."[75]

The Senators also criticized the executive's lack of assurance that the factors listed in the 1979 act had been considered before foreign policy controls were imposed; "The language of the act is intentionally flexible, but the report accompanying the latest extension of foreign policy controls gives little assurance that the criteria were ever adequately considered, hence our concern that the intent of the Congress is being circumvented. . . ."[76]

Nonetheless, five years later the Reagan administration sent a virtually identical Foreign Policy Report to Congress. The findings with regard to foreign availability of controlled commodities and the probability of achieving intended purposes through the use of controls were virtually unchanged from the Carter administration findings.[77] In short, the Reagan administration continued foreign policy controls regardless of foreign availability with little demonstration of the efficacy of such controls to Congress.

At the request of Congress, the General Accounting Office (GAO) considered the implementation of section 6 of the 1979 act, the foreign policy export control section, which required consideration of the domestic impact of such controls. The report specifically reviewed the Reagan administration's compliance with the 1979 act's provisions requiring (1) consultation, as appropriate, with business affected by the proposed controls, and (2) consideration of the economic impact of such controls before their implementation or expansion.

The report concluded that, despite the statutory recommendations, formal consultation with business did not generally take place. In the four instances mentioned above where the Reagan administration initiated or expanded export controls, the report found that formal business consultation occurred on only one occasion—the imposition of comprehensive export controls against Libya on March 12, 1982. These "consultations" were highly circumscribed and were merely pro forma affairs. The Commerce and State departments held a meeting with known and available U.S. exporters to Libya on March 4, 1982. Commerce extended the invitations to affected businesses one day before the meeting was held and did not inform potential participants of its purpose. Business groups were given one day, until March 5, to submit their comments. The business participants complained about the lack of time to submit adequate information and objected that the administration apparently had already decided to impose the controls. In the other three cases, the report found that either the administration made no attempt to consult with the American business community or that it placed last-minute phone calls to some American exporters. The administration justified its practices as necessary to avoid information leaks which might offset the impact of the controls and to prevent the target nation from taking measures to circumvent them.[78] Similarly, in the case of President Carter's controls following the invasion of Afghanistan, the administration did not hold discussions with the business community until weeks after announcing the policy.[79]

The GAO report also found that despite the Reagan administration's lack of formal consultation with the business community about the specific costs associated with a proposed control, the administration was aware of the business community's sentiments, including: (1) the doubtful effectiveness of unilateral U.S. export controls; (2) the need for close consultation and support from allied nations for controls to be effective; (3) the adverse consequences for American business resulting from the abrogation of existing contracts; (4) the damage to the reputation of American business as a reliable supplier and the possibility that they would be supplanted as suppliers by nations taking advantage of unilateral U.S. controls; and (5) the difficulty of removing controls once they were established.[80]

With respect to the specific issue of what economic cost information was developed by Commerce Department staff personnel and forwarded to the President or other decision-makers before controls were imposed, the report found that the administration had basic knowledge of direct export costs and the effect of the controls on some individual companies. In general, the report did not have the data to assess the controls' secondary effects, such as the consequences of future trade or the impact on subcontractors, jobs, and government revenues. Similarly, in making the annual foreign policy control extension review, the GAO found that the economic analysis conducted by the executive was usually perfunctory and did not represent a continuing effort to monitor adverse economic effects. In the report's estimation, the failure to measure the costs associated with established controls contributed to the difficulty of improving the calculation of economic effects, including secondary effects.[81]

In sum, the GAO study clarified one important point for Congress —it refuted the premise that the executive might have acted differently if it were aware of the probable costs. Although the President had not consulted with the business community as required by the 1979 act, the report found that the executive was generally aware of the direct costs and business concerns attending its policies, yet chose to impose controls *for its own foreign policy reasons*, despite the business community's opposition and the congressional restrictions. The report recommended, therefore, that Congress realize that the approach of the 1979 act to guide but not precisely limit presidential use of foreign policy export controls was essentially a failed one. If Congress were to conclude, as America's major trading partners and many scholars and policy analysts have, that unilateral foreign policy export controls are not an appropriate tool to achieve foreign policy goals, then it should, according to the GAO, eliminate this authority from the 1979 act rather than attempt to fine-tune the act to require that additional, more detailed criteria be considered.[82]

More recently, in 1983, a Senate report noted the "continued need to enhance consultation with industry on foreign policy controls."[83] The report expressed the need for the President to be held to a "stricter standard than has been the case heretofore, with regard to the justification for the imposition of foreign policy export controls."[84] In the case of the controls imposed in response to the declaration of martial law in Poland, the Senate acknowledged that the President had not seriously considered the factors set out in section 6(b) of the 1979 act.[85]

The executive also repeatedly ignored the requirement of the 1979 act that Congress be notified before export controls were imposed for foreign policy purposes.[86] For example, although President Reagan imposed additional foreign policy controls on exports to Libya on March 12, 1982, the Commerce Department did not notify and report to Congress until more than two months later.[87] The executive's disregard of the statutory requirements was even more apparent in the case of the expanded pipeline controls. On June 19, 1982, President Reagan directed that additional foreign policy controls be placed on exports of oil and gas exploration, production, transmission, and refining equipment and technical data to the Soviet Union. Although these controls were *terminated* on November 13, 1982, following a severe rift between the United States and its allies over the extraterritorial application of these controls, Congress was not notified of their *imposition* until November 29, 1982—two weeks after their termination.[88]

Congress recognized that the executive had not provided notification or reports to it as called for in the 1979 legislation. In a 1983 legislative session, the Senate stated that it was "dissatisfied with the degree of consultation that had been conducted by the current and past administrations with the Congress regarding the imposition, expansion, and extension of foreign policy export controls." Although the 1979 act requires that such consultation be conducted in every possible instance, the committee noted that meaningful consultation had been the exception rather than the rule.[89]

Congress was particularly concerned with the executive's failure to report to Congress in a timely and detailed fashion. For example, in hearings with representatives of the State and Commerce departments, Senator Heinz, the proponent of a reform export administration bill that nearly won passage in 1984, explained his motivations for the stricter reporting requirements his bill provided, again mentioning the pipeline case:

> Now let me give you a little of the thinking behind that. The report sent to Congress explaining the foreign policy controls with respect to the Soviet pipeline wasn't sent to Congress until after the controls on U.S. foreign subsidiaries and licen-

sees had already been lifted—that was 5 months after you imposed them. . . .

I am not trying to criticize you for the very late submission of the report. That's not the point. The point is how are we going to do it in the future? More importantly, the whole question is, before people jump in feet first to using foreign policy controls, what guarantees do we, as legislators, to our constituents and the people we all serve, including you, have that there is a thoughtful process which does make careful considerations and in some sense will meet the test?[90]

Consequently, Congress attempted to reform, via amending legislation, the reporting provision to require more frequent and more detailed demonstrations of compliance with the criteria of section 6.[91]

▪ Conclusion

This chapter has focused on the exercise of the executive's authority in foreign policy export control in the 1970s and early 1980s. Despite concerted effort, Congress failed to check the executive's use of this authority through passage of the 1979 act. Since that act, the executive has continued to fashion a foreign policy export control policy independent of both Congress's intent and its procedural requirements.

During the lawmaking process, the executive demonstrated many of the strengths that it had demonstrated in 1969 in negotiations with Congress over provisions of the 1979 act. Although Congress was far less divided over reform of foreign policy export controls in 1979 than it had been with regard to reform of national security export controls in 1969, it nonetheless lacked the executive's unity of position and the executive's ability to sustain its position over the course of the legislative process.

Unlike the 1969 period, in 1979 the executive relied on its historical and implied authority over foreign affairs as the basis for demanding that Congress not unduly limit its flexibility in the use of foreign policy export controls. In 1969, the executive had drawn in part on this source of authority during its negotiation with Congress, but had relied more heavily on its historic role in protecting national security and its institutional and technical expertise for resisting congressional attempts to limit its power.

In implementing foreign policy controls the executive consistently demonstrated a great deal of independence from Congress, interest groups, and international political constraints. The executive also exercised authority through its varied institutional and legal instruments. The Carter grain boycott, for example, was designated a national security as well as a foreign policy export control to preclude the possibility of a congressional veto over the use of foreign policy export controls to embargo agricultural commodities. As is discussed in the following chapter, President Reagan would use statutory authority under the International Emergency Economic Powers Act to similarly embargo agricultural exports to Nicaragua.

In summing up executive-congressional struggles over foreign policy export controls, one long-term insider to the process estimated that the executive possesses greater latitude vis-à-vis Congress in export controls (including the use of export controls for foreign policy, rather than national security, purposes) than in any other area of foreign economic policy. This estimation is in striking contrast to the conventional wisdom suggesting that congressional and interest group dominance or equivalence best characterizes U.S. trade policy, or that Congress has become increasingly assertive in foreign policy since the mid-1970s. Those who would dismiss executive preeminence as simply an aberration because of the latitude granted the executive in matters of national security must also explain away the executive's dominance in the use of the *foreign policy* export controls discussed in this chapter.

6. RECENT DEVELOPMENTS IN EXPORT POLICY

NEGOTIATIONS on the Export Administration Act of 1985 began in 1983. Although the House and Senate passed bills relatively early in 1983, conference negotiations to settle differences broke down after six months, and a final bill was never put to a vote.

The issue of export controls had become particularly divisive within Congress and within the executive between pro-export forces and those committed to denying high-technology items to the Eastern bloc. Difficulty in reaching a legislative compromise in 1983–84 is attributable in significant part to these divisions, as well as to clashes between the administration and Congress or the business community.

The Senate bill, S. 979, was a carefully crafted compromise between John Heinz, chairman of the International Finance and Monetary Policy Subcommittee, who pushed for stricter limits on the use of export controls for foreign policy purposes, and Jake Garn, Banking Committee chairman, who sought tighter export controls to protect U.S. national security. Varying coalitions in the Senate adopted provisions to tighten controls over nuclear-related exports, expand the role of the Defense Department in reviewing exports to COCOM and nonaligned Western nations, enhance the enforcement authority of the Customs Service, curtail the President's authority to impose foreign policy controls on U.S. agricultural exports, and prevent the President from breaching existing contracts when imposing foreign policy controls.

The House bill, H.R. 3231, whose chief sponsor was Don Bonker (D-Wash.), sought to liberalize licensing requirements for exports to COCOM, retain exclusive authority for review of West-West licensing in the Commerce Department, maintain primary enforcement responsibility in the Commerce Department, and require a congressional role in any presidential decision to extend foreign policy controls extraterritorially.

The administration generally opposed any restrictions on its authority to use export controls for foreign policy reasons, although there was some sentiment in the State Department for limiting the extraterritorial reach of foreign policy export controls. The primary battle within the administration, however, was the jurisdictional dispute over West-West licensing between the Commerce and Defense departments. The White House did not favor the Senate bill—which reassigned a portion of West-West licensing review authority to the Defense Department—viewing resolution of the dispute as an executive prerogative rather than a congressional one. The Commerce Department, led by Under Secretary of Commerce Lionel Olmer, and the Defense Department, led by Assistant Secretary of Defense Richard Perle, conflicted violently over this issue and over enforcement questions.

Ultimately, the licensing review dispute between the Defense and Commerce departments was settled through an ancillary agreement. The Reagan administration adopted guidelines detailing the scope of Defense Department authority in reviewing export license applications for high-technology shipments to noncommunist nations. In a January 1985 directive, the administration implemented an earlier decision which granted the Defense Department authority in principle to participate in the Commerce Department's review of "distribution licenses," which permit multiple shipment of goods to noncommunist countries. This authority was conditioned on successful implementation of a memorandum of understanding between the two agencies for Defense Department review of individual licenses for West-West trade involving selective countries and commodities.[1]

The business community, in contrast to the administration and Congress, agreed on basic principles for revising the export control laws, including the need to recognize the sanctity of contracts, limit or prohibit the extraterritorial application of foreign policy controls, improve consultation between the executive and Congress before imposition of foreign policy controls, and prohibit an increase in Defense Department authority in licensing exports.

The U.S. business community lobbied Congress strenuously over the 1985 act. Business leaders directed much of their effort at reforming the foreign policy provisions. In general, business interests continued to criticize foreign policy controls as unpredictable, costly, and generally ineffective in achieving their stated aims.[2] The business community believed that the existing criteria the President must consider before imposing such controls needed to be strengthened by requiring a more compelling demonstration of need, effectiveness, and foreign unavailability. Business spokesmen uniformly opposed unilateral U.S. foreign policy export controls on goods freely available from foreign suppliers, as well as the retroactive implementation of foreign policy controls, which in the past had permitted the President to break existing contracts. Furthermore, several spokesmen for the business community strongly recommended that foreign policy controls not be applied extraterritorially to restrict the practices of foreign nationals, including subsidiaries and licensees of U.S. corporations.

Although a compromise bill could not be reached in 1984, the following year, Representative Don Bonker and Senator John Heinz put the legislation on a fast track by proposing a new bill that contained the 1984 conference agreements and by deleting two controversial issues which had derailed the legislation in the prior session: sanctions against South Africa and the Defense Department's role in reviewing "West-West" export licenses.

As a result, after two and a half years of congressional deliberation, on July 12, 1985, President Reagan signed into law the Export Administration Amendments Act of 1985.[3] This new law constituted an amendment and reauthorization of the Export Administration Act of 1979. The 1985 act changed prior law in a number of significant respects, including:

- providing that the President make certain determinations and consult with Congress in a more meaningful way before imposing foreign policy export controls;
- providing a measure of immunity for existing contracts from foreign policy export controls;
- placing limitations on the Commerce Department's authority to deny an application for an export license for a commodity or technology, if comparable goods or technologies were readily available from foreign sources;
- eliminating the need for export licenses on certain "low-technology" items (e.g., personal computers) destined for COCOM countries, and requiring expedited processing of applications for licenses to export other controlled goods or technology to those countries; and

—shortening the processing times for export license applications.

In many respects the 1985 act reflected the concerns of the business community and those in Congress who sought to liberalize U.S. export controls. For example, the 1985 act contained a new provision prohibiting retroactive revocation of existing contracts by imposition of foreign policy controls (the so-called "contract sanctity" provision). Furthermore, in situations where foreign availability of a controlled product existed, foreign policy export controls unilaterally imposed by the United States were limited to six months in duration.

As in earlier instances, however, these "successes" may be more nominal than actual. The contract sanctity provision, for example, allows the executive to avoid its restrictions whenever the President determines and certifies that a breach of the peace poses a serious and direct threat to the strategic interests of the United States. This certification requirement, like other congressional requirements for executive reports, determinations, and findings, appears unlikely to deter the executive from imposing foreign policy controls which could sever preexisting contracts.

Moreover, many of the changes in the foreign policy section of the 1985 act seem to be little more than semantic. For example, the requirement for "considerations" before imposition of foreign policy export controls was changed to "determinations." Congress strengthened this provision because it believed the executive had ignored the message contained in the 1979 act; that the executive must carefully weigh the cost and consider alternatives before imposing controls. Yet, Congress again deferred to executive foreign affairs authority in not placing stricter limits on executive discretion; thus, it is highly unlikely that this provision will impose any real restraint on executive authority.

In fact, although the 1985 act limits the use of foreign policy controls to situations where the executive has determined the impact, significance, and effectiveness of proposed controls and reported his determinations to Congress, a 1986 study by the GAO found the Commerce Department's report to Congress on foreign policy export controls in that year deficient in meeting many of these reporting requirements.[4] The GAO concluded that the executive's assessment of alternative means for achieving the purposes of foreign policy controls and the ability of the United States to enforce its controls were insufficient. The GAO further found the

Commerce Department's assessments of alternative means "generally contain declarative sentences with little or no explanation."[5] The report added:

> Because in our view, the [foreign policy] controls extended by the Secretary [of Commerce] are mostly symbolic and generally impose few, if any, costs on the countries which are the targets of the controls while imposing costs on American businesses, we believe it is especially important to examine alternatives. Consequently, we believe that more complex reporting on the secretary's consideration of symbolic export controls will assist the Congress in its oversight of the Department of Commerce's implementation of the 1985 Act.[6]

The report specifically recommended a fuller discussion of alternative means considered and a statement as to why alternatives were determined to be unsuitable.[7]

In other respects, efforts to liberalize the export control laws were not translated into reforms of the foreign policy provisions of the 1985 act. For example, Congress did not alter the provision governing the extraterritorial application of U.S. foreign policy export control laws. Representative Bonker's bill aspired to limit the application of export controls to goods and technology produced in the United States, but the House-Senate conference receded from this position in view of executive opposition.[8] Similarly, Bonker abandoned plans for subjecting the reviewing agencies to judicial scrutiny under the Administrative Procedures Act when he encountered administrative opposition and congressional reluctance, on grounds that the proposal constituted a congressional or judicial infringement on the executive's foreign affairs and national security powers.

In the area of national security, Congress eliminated licensing requirements for exports of relatively low-technology items and accelerated processing deadlines for exports of high-technology items to COCOM countries. In other particulars, the national security provisions rewritten by Congress may prove less than reformers had hoped.

Despite Congress's efforts to eliminate unilateral controls when the controlled good or technology is available from foreign sources, the 1985 act continues to provide a loophole for executive discretion. The act appears to add more stringent foreign availability assessment provisions to the national security section. Specifically, the 1985 act authorized the Technical Advisory Committees to make initial determinations of foreign availability of specific commodities; these commodities must be decontrolled unless the Department of Commerce rebuts the evidence within 90 days. In addition, the legislation requires that the Commerce Department accept an applicant's representations regarding foreign availability if supported by "reasonable evidence" and grant an export license unless the department has "reliable" contrary evidence.

These efforts, however, are vitiated by the concurrent grant of authority to the President to maintain controls for up to 18 months, despite a finding of foreign availability under the act. The executive will thus maintain the ability to ignore foreign availability findings should it choose to do so.

Institutional barriers to decontrolling commodities because of foreign availability also remain formidable obstacles to reform. Although the Commerce Department's Office of Foreign Availability began assessments and improved its data-gathering abilities in 1985, interdepartmental (i.e., Commerce-Defense-State) consensus on implementing the letter and spirit of the law was clearly lacking.[9] Consequently, as of 1987, the Commerce Department had made only one published, positive finding of foreign availability.[10] The finding applied to automatic wafering saws used to slice silicon for computer chips. The Commerce Department's finding removed unilateral U.S. controls on the West-West export of the wafering saws. Nonetheless, the Defense Department remained opposed to the decontrol and stalled the West-East multilateral decontrol procedure in COCOM.[11] At a 1986 congressional hearing, Talbot Lindstrom, Deputy Director of the Defense Department Defense Technology Security Administration, maintained that Defense recommended against decontrol of the wafering saws and he left open the possibility that Defense would attempt to scuttle the decontrol effort in COCOM.[12]

Finally, the 1985 act makes a number of changes intended to expedite the processing of applications for export licenses. The new timetable attempts to reduce most deadlines by one-third. While this effort may have some salutary effect on the efficiency of license processing, there are strong reasons to believe that delays will continue. The Department of Commerce released figures which reveal that as of January 17, 1986, 2,131 applications with a reported value of almost $1.9 billion were pending at the Commerce Department beyond their statutory deadline for action. The vast majority of the delayed cases, 1,920 applications, were pending for over 120 days, despite the 60-day processing deadline.[13]

The issues before Congress during the two and one-half years spent reauthorizing and amending the Export Administration Act should now ring familiar. Congress, at the urging of the business community, addressed provisions governing the assessment of foreign availability, the executive's discretion in using foreign policy and national security controls, the processing of licenses, and the act's jurisdictional scope.

Because of divisions within Congress over the preferred course of reform and congressional deference to the executive's national security and foreign affairs authority, the legislative outcome also reflects a pattern whereby congressional efforts were embodied in several statutory reforms, but often in ways that were ultimately unlikely to prohibit the executive's use of its own discretion.

The most recent congressional efforts have not been appreciably more effective than previous attempts. In instances where the executive's interest in the use of export controls differed from that of Congress or the business community, the executive was not impeded by the 1985 act.[14]

The Reagan administration undertook a variety of policies immediately before and after passage of the 1985 act that continued to demonstrate a great deal of executive autonomy and capacity in the use of export controls for foreign policy purposes. The most important were embargoes against Nicaragua and Libya. The President implemented both these policies under the International Emergency Economic Powers Act (IEEPA), rather than the Export Administration Act. The President invoked his authority under IEEPA in the case of Nicaragua because the Export Administration Act had expired and its provisions had been maintained through a presidential declaration of national emergency and the invocation of IEEPA. The President subsequently extended that embargo several times. President Reagan imposed sanctions against Libya under IEEPA allegedly because the use of IEEPA may have been more appropriate than the 1985 act for implementing a total embargo, and the use of the IEEPA allowed the President to avoid the contract sanctity provisions and the prohibition on the use of foreign policy export controls for agricultural products in the 1985 act.

Moreover, the Nicaraguan embargo decision was a clear demonstration of executive independence from Congress, domestic interest groups, and U.S. allies. The presidential embargo on Nicaragua carried out under IEEPA followed closely a House rejection on April 25, 1985 of President Reagan's proposal for $14 million in military aid for Nicaraguan rebels. The President's actions provoked allied opposition announced during the 1985 economic summit in Bonn, strong opposition from other Central American nations, concern in the American business community, particularly from U.S. agricultural exporters, and, at best, a mixed reaction in Congress.[15] The executive, in announcing the Nicaraguan embargo, again ignored the act's requirement that the executive consult with Congress.[16]

Some members of Congress viewed use of the IEEPA to implement the Libyan embargo, rather than the foreign policy provision of the newly enacted Export Administration Amendments Act, as a means for the executive to avoid the new foreign policy restrictions. Although the Reagan administration justified its use of IEEPA on grounds that it was a more appropriate statutory instrument than the Export Administration Act for total embargoes, Representative Don Bonker informed former Secretary of Commerce Malcolm Baldrige that he considered it an affront that the President had bypassed the express wishes of Congress through his use of the IEEPA.[17]

Both the Libyan and Nicaraguan embargoes reflect the strength, initiative, and multiple instrumentalities of the executive. The strengthening of controls against South Africa, however, presents a more atypical case in which Congress was the motivating force for foreign policy export controls.

In 1985, the President, who had opposed additional export controls against South Africa, when faced with the prospect that Congress would pass a sanctions bill, effectively fashioned a program of limited export controls and other punitive measures, thereby heading off congressional demands for stronger measures.[18] In essence, the President's export control authority was used in a preemptive way to fashion a second-best policy.

The President's South African policy ran aground the following year. In perhaps the most important foreign policy defeat of the Reagan presidency, Congress enacted a law imposing economic sanctions against South Africa.[19] President Reagan had vetoed the bill on September 26, 1986, but both Houses voted to override the veto, the House on September 29 and the Senate on October 2. Although the bill did not expand the export restraints imposed by President Reagan in 1985, it imposed several additional economic sanctions[20] and represented a clear rebuke of the executive's policy. The South African sanctions were, by their unprecedented nature, an exception that proves the rule that export sanctions are policy instruments primarily under control of the executive.

Conclusion

Passage of the 1985 act and the executive's subsequent policy initiatives are generally consistent with the pattern of relations between the executive, Congress, and interest groups in making export control law and policy discussed in earlier chapters. Congress was generally unable to confront the executive in crafting legislative language that would significantly reform the national security or foreign policy provisions of the 1985 act.

As was the case in 1969, divisions within Congress over reform legislation stalemated several initiatives. The executive's inability to present coherent, relatively unified demands to Congress with regard to several proposed amendments was unique to passage of the 1985 act. However, the executive's indecisiveness contributed more to confusion and delay than to strengthening the hand of Congress. Furthermore, as in prior legislative engagements, the executive's established authority in foreign affairs and national security and its specific institutional expertise in administering export controls constrained Congress's efforts to respond to the demands of the U.S. exporting community.

Implementation of U.S. export control policy since passage of the 1985 act does not suggest any significant departures from previous practices. As noted, licensing delays persisted, the assessment of foreign availability moved at glacial speed, and the President imposed foreign policy controls largely independent of domestic or congressional concerns.

7. PATTERNS OF EXECUTIVE AUTHORITY

DESPITE periodic attention to the exceptional uses of U.S. export control policy as a tool of economic coercion, political scientists have not focused on the origins, operations, and enduring features of the U.S. export control system. Existing theoretic approaches to U.S. foreign policy or trade policy do not fully explain U.S. export controls. Furthermore, although the prevailing understanding of U.S. foreign policy anticipates executive branch dominance, especially in matters of national security, it fails to account for the emergence and continuation of the executive's dominance in the use of foreign policy export controls in the 1970s and 1980s, a time when Congress was reasserting itself in matters of foreign policy generally.

Pluralist approaches correctly recognize that American business interests have an immediate and considerable stake in export controls. Moreover, pluralism is indispensable to explanations of certain export policies and a necessary element to understanding the operations of the current system. Nonetheless, unlike U.S. import policy, export policy cannot be explained convincingly by pluralism alone. Theories that explicitly or implicitly apply pluralist explanations to U.S. export control policy fail to account for the repeated pattern of executive dominance over Congress and interest groups that has been documented in this book.

This book argues that an appreciation of the role of the executive and executive institutions is necessary to understand U.S. export control policy. The executive is more than merely a player, among many, in shaping export controls. Executive institutions exert an enduring influence over the making and implementation of policy and are largely unaffected by the waxing and waning of presidential influence in Congress.

What role do the executive and its institutions play in this area? Certain patterns have emerged over forty years of U.S. export controls. First, the lawmaking process often reveals a clash of executive and congressional interests. Although policy differences have existed between agencies and within Congress (especially of late), the executive has generally presented a unified front in expressing statutory preferences distinct from those of the congressional majority. Contrary to the congressional emphasis on making the export control system more efficient and accountable, and its use as a tool of general foreign policy exceptional, the executive has stressed the need to use export controls to further its national security and foreign policy goals. Moreover, during the lawmaking process, the executive has been able to prevail on Congress to modify legislation so that executive authority and flexibility would not be significantly altered.

The sources of executive strength and influence over Congress during the legislative process are numerous. Although various executive departments and agencies have different attitudes toward export control policy, the executive is more able to coalesce around a legislative strategy and pursue that strategy than those in Congress seeking to change policy. Executive department cohesion is assisted greatly by a clear indication from the White House on the course of U.S. export policy. The salutary affects of White House leadership were evidenced during passage of the 1969 Export Administration Act. Lack of White House leadership in the 1980s contributed to executive department infighting (particularly between the departments of Commerce and Defense) and thereby complicated the lawmaking process.

In addition to a greater singleness of purpose than Congress, the executive possesses a host of other means by which it can shape export control legislation, including partisan influence in Congress, a historic and constitutional role in protecting U.S. national security and furthering U.S. foreign policy interests, and superior technical expertise and experience in export control administration.[1] Foreign policy export control authority is a noteworthy example wherein executive prerogatives successfully defended during the lawmaking process were subsequently employed by the executive in fashioning an independent policy.

In implementing policy, the executive has repeatedly, in Cohen's words, transcended particular interests and sacrificed the goal of wealth maximization through free trade for national security and foreign policy.[2] The pursuit of national security and foreign policy interests has meant different things to different administrations. The Carter administration included the promotion of human rights as an essential goal to be furthered through the use of export controls, whereas the Reagan administration was more concerned with combating international terrorism by this means. Export controls employed for national security purposes have also meant different things to the same administration at different times. In its first term, for example, the Nixon administration used export controls to embargo most East-West trade as a means of denying U.S. goods and technology to the Soviet Union, thereby serving the national security interests of the United States. In its second term, the Nixon administration relaxed U.S. export controls on nonstrategic trade when it redefined national security to include expanded East-West contacts as part of its policy of détente.

The executive's pursuit of various goals should not confuse a more basic fact; the executive consistently used export controls to serve self-defined goals, despite the domestic and international opposition that attended many of these policies. Nowhere has the relatively high level of executive autonomy been more apparent than in the executive's increasing use of foreign policy export controls, beginning in the late 1970s. The embargoes implemented against Nicaragua and Libya and the South African sanctions suggest that executive autonomy in this area is likely to continue for the foreseeable future.

Furthermore, executive institutions have pursued distinctive goals and realized them in varying degrees. In contrast to the post-1969 congressional emphasis on export expansion, executive institutions throughout the 1970s have consistently limited exports that *they believed* could endanger national security. Institutional practices reflected less concern than Congress displayed with the competitive detriment export licensing posed for American exporters. This institutional orientation was formed during more than twenty years of implementing an export embargo against Communist countries and is illustrated in the manner in which executive institutions resisted the reforms mandated by Congress in the 1969 act and the amendments to the Export Administration Act in the 1970s and 1980s.

The origins of the executive's authority, institutional and otherwise, can be traced to its wartime emergency powers, retained and expanded during two decades of U.S. hegemony, Cold War rivalry, and executive–congressional–interest-group congruence on the purposes to be served by U.S. export controls. The executive has used its originally delegated authority to establish an elaborate and insulated export control apparatus.

The nature of the system has enabled it to preserve its autonomy and resist many societal demands for change. Export controls are a policy arena particularly susceptible to institutional control and highly resistant to outside pressure for reform. Export controls monitor all exported civilian goods and technology. The resources needed to administer this inclusive system are necessarily vast and complex. Numerous bureaucracies are involved in making thousands of individual, highly technical rulings on the export of particular goods or technology to particular destinations. Moreover, the institutions making these decisions are not accountable either electorally, through oversight, or in the courts.

Executive institutions have been slow to change. In part, this rigidity can be attributed to the difficulty of translating statutory directives into meaningful change when institutional practices are well-entrenched and the institutions are largely unaccountable to those mandating change. Moreover, the mandates themselves—the statutes—harbor many ambiguities and ill-resolved compromises, perhaps none greater than the dual purpose of the act—to expand U.S. exports while protecting national security.

Institutional structures and practices also foreclose the possibility of certain internal reforms. For example, export license processing may be "system limited" because different executive departments with varying mandates and vested interests in the existing system, coupled with the case-by-case method of licensing, prohibit more expeditious license processing. Absent a fundamental change in one or more of these institutional features, significant reform is unlikely, if not impossible.

In short, the executive and its institutions have defined relatively autonomous interests in the domestic lawmaking process, and executive policies reveal significant capacity to prevail over domestic preferences in the implementation of policy. This book has endeavored to demonstrate the executive's autonomy and capacity, document the sources of executive authority, and distill the content of its policies and procedures in an important, but often overlooked, aspect of U.S. foreign economic policy.

In addition to qualifying pluralist assumptions about trade policy, how might this understanding of executive dominance and the importance of executive institutions fit with theoretical notions of U.S. foreign policy? James Rosenau identified five categories of explanatory variables for foreign policy; systemic (external), societal, governmental, role, and individual factors.[3] These categories are offered as exhaustive and mutually exclusive factors shaping foreign policy behavior. For a large country with an open policy and a developed economy (such as the United States), in a "nonhuman resource" policy where both the means and the ends of policy are tangible (such as East-West trade), Rosenau ranks these variables by their explanatory potency as follows: (1) role variables; (2) systemic variables; (3) societal variables; (4) governmental variables; and (5) individual variables.

Clearly, this book affirms the importance of role variables. The executive's dominant role vis-à-vis Congress in U.S. export control policy is a central contention of this book. Furthermore, these roles, once established, are a persistent feature of export control policy.

Equally apparent, Rosenau's model underestimates the importance of government organizations in shaping export control policy. Graham Allison's "Model II," which understands government behavior less as deliberate choices of leaders and more as outputs of large organizations functioning according to standard patterns of behavior, also appears directly relevant.[4]

As the organizational paradigm would predict, fractionalized power in export control administration encourages organizational parochialism. This attitude and approach, when coupled with standard operating procedures and negotiated solutions to policy questions, results in persistent, inflexible policies not easily disturbed by the intervention of government leaders and likely to change only incrementally, if at all.[5]

At the conclusion of a study, often one discovers as many questions as answers. This book has attempted to illustrate through a systematic study of postwar U.S. export control policy the pattern of executive dominance in the use of national security and foreign policy export controls. It has also explained the surprising degree of continuity in this policy despite rising business discontent (stemming from the vastly increased importance of exports to the U.S. economy), the end of the Cold War consensus, and a resurgence in congressional influence in foreign policy generally.

Part of the answer, it has been suggested, is the enduring practices of insulated, largely unaccountable bureaucracies whose policies rarely resemble those called for by Congress. Extensive discussion has been devoted to establishing that these bureaucratic organizations persist and describing the manner in which they shape export control policy. Why the practices of the Commerce Department's Office of Export Administration persist despite the repeatedly expressed ire of congressional committees and the Commerce Department's business constituency is not fully addressed here.

The organizational politics model may offer a partial answer. That model suggests a variety of factors that encourage organizational parochialism and persistence, including (1) selective information available to the organization, (2) recruitment of personnel into the organization, (3) tenure of individuals in the organization, (4) small group pressures within the organization, (5) distribution of rewards by the organization, and (6) reinforcement from clients (e.g., interest groups) and government allies (e.g., congressional committees).[6] Two of these factors, selectively available information and small group pressures for conformity, clearly are relevant to an explanation of why certain export control policies endure.

One factor, reinforcement, however, raises other questions. If the Office of Export Administration in the Commerce Department frequently operates in a manner at odds with the desires of its traditional interest group (business) and is simultaneously attacked in Congress, by export "liberals" as slow, inefficient, and burdensome to business and by export "conservatives" as inadequate in enforcement matters, who, then, are its constituent and government allies? One could speculate that, ironically, its rival agencies, particularly the Department of Defense, offer important protection and purpose to the interagency mediator role played by the Commerce Department's Office of Export Administration.

Similarly, the ability of the executive to maintain an expansive national security export control list despite strong societal pressures for liberalization, worldwide availability of many controlled products, and possible erosion of U.S. economic and military capabilities as the consequence of excessive controls is also a question that cannot be answered fully here. This study does suggest certain elements of an explanation, however. For example, the original orientation of the system (an embargo of Communist countries), the inherent conservatism of incremental, interagency, and consensual decision-making regarding list reduction, and the general insulation of the entire system from business input or judicial scrutiny facilitate the continuation of established policies.

In addition, public choice theory may be of some use in explaining these phenomena. Public choice theory assumes that policymakers pursue public policy goals consistent with their personal welfare and, to a lesser degree, are motivated by interpersonal or social concerns. Nonelected export control bureaucrats, be they in the Defense, Commerce, or State departments, benefit immediately and directly in terms of job security and promotion and avoid risk by the continuation of policies that promote a conservative export control bureaucracy. For example, the personal career risk a government bureaucrat faces in reaching a licensing decision stems solely from allowing a strategic export. Because there is no accountability to the exporter, the bureaucrat is generally not at risk in disallowing a nonstrategic export. Thus, in the event of uncertainty, the export bureaucracy will deny a license if forced to decide.

Furthermore, not only is a bureaucracy's welfare increased by a large and conservative export control system, but its social and interpersonal goals are also served by the existing system. For example, self-interest in maintaining the export control system is bolstered by an interpersonal value—respect for the status quo—and social concerns—the belief that this traditional approach to export control policy promotes the collective good of national security.[7]

This book cannot hope to answer fully these and other questions. The peacetime U.S. export control system has survived largely unaltered for over forty years. The system and these questions are likely to be around a good while longer.

The history of U.S. export control policy counsels caution in anticipating change in the system. If change is sought—to redress America's huge trade deficits and its evaporating surplus in high-technology trade during an era when technological advancement is no longer driven by defense procurement or exclusively under American control—then an understanding of the organization of power in export controls is required.

NOTES

1. A Theory of U.S. Export Control Policy

1. *Balancing the National Interest*, p. 121.
2. In fiscal year 1986, the Commerce Department received almost 115,000 export and reexport license applications, with over 102,000 involving noncommunist destinations.
3. Literature on American economic coercion focuses primarily on the effectiveness of the more extreme cases of export sanctions. It generally takes the form of a cost-benefit analysis of unilateral American boycotts or sanctions implemented under U.S. export control laws or an analysis of a multilateral boycott with American participation.

The historical attitude of political scientists toward U.S. economic coercion implemented under U.S. export control laws or under international law has undergone several changes. After World War I, sanctions were viewed as a viable, effective means of resolving international differences short of the use of force. By the late 1960s, however, economic sanctions were in disrepute. Although such policies were seen as costly to the target state, their political, economic, and legal consequences to the sender state (usually the United States) were also considered significant.

Current literature on American economic coercion questions the assumption that economic coercion does not work. The most recent studies suggest that while a sanction usually fails to influence significantly the policies of the nation toward which it is directed, it may serve a variety of lesser goals without incurring the costs associated with military intervention. This fact, combined with the demands of political expediency or the lack of policy alternatives, may explain the repeated resort to economic coercive policies. For the most recent and systematic rethinking of the use and usefulness of economic sanctions see David A. Baldwin, *Economic Statecraft;* and Gary Clyde Hufbauer and Jeffrey J. Schott, with Kimberly Ann Elliott, *Economic Sanctions Reconsidered: History and Current Policy.*

4. For purposes of this book, the executive—the President, the appointed heads of the relevant executive agencies, and the bureaucracy—is contrasted with Congress, interest groups, and individuals.

Prior studies of U.S. foreign economic policy similarly distinguish the executive from Congress and interest groups, and the state from its society. For example, Graham Allison and Peter Szanton define the executive as a series of institutions emanating in a concentric pattern from the President: "Just beyond the White House lies the Executive Office of the President, the institutional presidency. . . . The third circle is the appointive government. The several hundred secretaries, under secretaries, assistant secretaries, and their deputies who comprise the administration expect to direct the departments, linking the President with the operating levels of government. . . . Finally, there is the permanent government. The more than three million people (some two million of them military) who did not change with the Presidents, but carry on the day-to-day work of all administrations." Having defined the executive, the authors then sharply differentiate the executive from Congress, interest groups and individuals: "Beyond the executive branch—which for all its unwieldiness at least is [the President's] . . .—lies Congress, alien territory. Beyond that, the private sector of the economy, another participant in the making and execution of foreign policy; and beyond that the larger public. . . ." Allison and Szanton; *Remaking Foreign Policy: The Organizational Connection,* pp. 64, 65.

Similarly, Stephen Krasner in *Defending the National Interest* defines the central state actors as the President and the heads of the relevant executive agencies. Krasner adds that while the distinction between state and society "does not mean to imply that a state's objectives are unrelated to the needs of its society . . . at the same time . . . it is a fundamental error to identify the goals of the state with some summation of the desire of specific individuals or groups." (pp. 11–12).

5. It is not surprising that pluralism, the modern variant of liberalism, should be offered as an explanation for U.S. export control policy. David Baldwin notes that liberalism dominates Anglo-American thinking in the area of foreign economic policy in particular. The liberal assumption that governmental management of economic relations should be minimal and the "pervasive ideology that sanctifies the independence, rather than the subordination, of economic power to government," contributes, in Baldwin's estimation, to the lack of academic attention to economic statecraft in Great Britain and the United States. Baldwin, *Economic Statecraft,* p. 59.

6. Furthermore, Theodore Lowi's refinement of the pluralist model suggests that pluralism is particularly relevant to explaining "regulatory policies." Regulatory policies are distinguishable from distribu-

tive policies in that they involve raising costs and/or reducing or expanding alternatives of private individuals. Regulatory policies allegedly fit the pluralist model of policymaking because varied interests battle for influence and input into the policymaking process centered in Congress. Export control policy is a clear example of a regulatory policy. In export control policy, Congress channels and articulates, via legislation, particular domestic interests in a highly politicized policy arena. See Theodore J. Lowi, "American Business, Public Policy, Case-Studies, and Political Theory."

7. Gary K. Bertsch, "American Politics and Trade with the USSR," in Bruce Parrott, ed., *Trade, Technology, and Soviet-American Relations*, pp. 244–45.

8. *Ibid.*, p. 277.

9. *Ibid.*

10. Political scientists focus more on import than export policies and characterize U.S. trade policy as the "stuff of domestic interests" in which Congress links trade policy to the wishes of particular domestic groups. Joan Edelman Spero, *The Politics of International Economic Relations*, p. 91. For example, the comprehensive and insightful book by Raymond Bauer, Ithiel de Sola Pool, and Lewis Dexter, *American Business and Public Policy*, analyzed trade policymaking, but concentrated on congressional decision-making and business-congressional relations rather than on the role of the executive. See also E. E. Schattschneider, *Politics, Pressures, and the Tariff*. Similarly, Krasner described the American state as weak when compared to central state actors in Japan or even France or Great Britain in formulating trade policy. Stephen D. Krasner, "United States Commercial and Monetary Policy: Unravelling the Paradox of External Strength and Internal Weakness," p. 87. See also Krasner, *Defending the National Interest*, p. 343.

11. Benjamin J. Cohen, ed., *American Foreign Economic Policy*, p. 20.

12. *Ibid.*

13. Robert A. Pastor, "The Cry-and-Sigh Syndrome: Congress and Trade Policy," p. 160.

14. Pastor, "The Cry-and-Sigh Syndrome," p. 188. See also Harold Malmgren, "A Historical View of Congress's Impact on Trade Legislation," in *Congress and U.S. Trade Policy* (Dallas: LTV Corporation, 1983), pp. 49–62.

15. Pastor, 'The Cry-and-Sigh Syndrome," p. 164. A more recent, and more accurate characterization of U.S. import policy is offered by economist Robert Baldwin. Baldwin notes the limitations that attend explanations of trade policy as governmental responses to political pressure from various groups "whose members are attempting to maximize their shortrun gains from trade by influencing public policy."

Rather, given the authority and responsibilities that the President and the International Trade Commission have accrued in import policy, many trade policy initiatives, in Baldwin's estimation, are better explained by an approach which emphasizes that "governmental officials are also regarded as having some scope to follow their own public policy preferences." Robert E. Baldwin, *The Political Economy of U.S. Import Policy*.

16. Pastor notes that foreign policymaking does not fit the simple mold of the President proposing and the Congress disposing. For example, procedural changes devised and written into the Trade Agreements Act of 1974 by Congress ensured active congressional involvement in every stage of subsequent negotiations. Section 151 of the Trade Act of 1974 established a "fast track" procedure for consideration of legislation to implement the subsequent Tokyo Round agreements which became the Trade Agreements Act of 1979.

Section 151 precluded legislative amendment of the final agreement and required that Congress accept or reject the legislation within 60 days. This fast track procedure was and is important in gaining swift enactment of complex trade agreements and in giving a reasonable expectation to the President and foreign governments involved that any trade agreement eventually negotiated will become U.S. law in the form in which it is agreed upon by the parties. While this procedure restricts Congress from responding to pressures to amend the implementing legislation, Pastor asserts it also means that no complex trade agreement subject to this procedure is possible absent a congressional mandate and active congressional involvement from start to finish.

Consequently, during negotiation of the Trade Agreements Act of 1979, Robert Strauss, President Carter's Special Trade Representative, took care to consult congressional leaders throughout the negotiation. Actual passage of the bill involved Congress drafting the bill, the executive having the responsibility of final revision and amendment, and Congress voting to accept or reject it. Pastor concludes that "the Trade Agreements Act of 1979 reflected the refinement of an informal and trusting relationship between the branches on trade policy into a formal procedure," and that should "the executive fail to negotiate in a way that reflects congressional concerns one might expect Congress to reduce the executive's negotiating authority and discretion, as it has done on foreign aid." Pastor, 'The Cry-and-Sigh Syndrome," pp. 178–84.

17. See, for example, Holbert N. Carroll, *The House of Representatives and Foreign Affairs*, pp. 4–8; Robert A. Dahl, *Congress and Foreign Policy*, p. 58; James A. Robinson, *Congress and Foreign Policy-Making*, p. v.

18. Dahl, *Congress and Foreign Policy*, p. 58.

19. *Ibid.*

20. Robinson, *Congress and Foreign Policy-Making*, p. 7.

21. Louis Henkin, in summarizing Congress's and the executive's respective jurisdictions over foreign affairs wrote: "The President largely makes foreign policy, even if Congress and Congressmen do not refrain from telling him what it ought to be. There is generally little disposition ever to challenge his uses of troops for foreign relations purposes where they are not likely to become involved in fighting. At the other end of the axis, Congress alone clearly adopts domestic legislation, regulates foreign commerce, authorizes spending and appropriates money and—happily not often—makes war." Louis Henkin, *Foreign Affairs and the Constitution*, pp. 271–72.

22. *Ibid.* Furthermore, American economic and political philosophy generally places a unique emphasis on the Constitution and rule of law rather than on institutions. The Constitution was designed to guard against a centralized state; federal powers were limited, with all residual authority vested in the states, and individuals and federal powers were split among three coequal branches each with the ability to restrain the others. In the area of economic regulation in particular, the founding fathers feared the power of the federal government. By constitutional design, public economic welfare was not to be the province of the American state but was left to the aggregation of private preferences.

23. See Kenneth C. MacKenzie, *Tariff-Making and Trade Policy in the U.S. and Canada*. MacKenzie notes that "the executive branch did make a number of attempts to enter into agreements with other countries for reciprocal reductions in customs duties, but most were frustrated in the Senate" (p. 1).

24. 48 Stat. 943 (1934).

25. As was noted earlier, more important than constitutional or legal limitations are the practical and political limits thought to attend the President's ability to make trade policy. Most complex international trade agreements require a statutory delegation of negotiating authority, implementing legislation, and appropriations; therefore, they necessarily require active involvement by both houses of Congress. Without Congress's political mandate in the form of a statutory delegation of trade-negotiating authority, the promise of speedy implementation, and the provision of sufficient appropriations, major trade initiatives are thought to be politically impossible. See Pastor, *Congress and the Politics of U.S. Foreign Economic Policy*; Pastor, "The 'Cry-and-Sigh' Syndrome."

In these respects, export control policy appears no different than other areas of U.S. trade policy: Congress delegates authority for a limited period of time to the executive, passes and, more often than not, initiates export control legislation, and appropriates funds for implementation and administration.

26. These hypotheses are more in keeping with recent work from both the realist and Marxist perspectives. For example, Krasner argues for the power of a "statist" approach to explaining foreign policy. This approach assumes the state is an autonomous actor that pursues ideologically determined objectives which "cannot be reduced to some summation of private desires." Krasner terms the state's objectives "the national interest." Similarly, Theda Skocpol suggests that the state may be independent of the interests of both capital and labor and that the state's motivation is more likely to be self-preservation than the predetermined service of a particular economic interest.

These recent theories capture on one level the nature of U.S. export control policy. It will be seen that when the nation's security, ideological, or foreign policy interest clashed with narrow economic interest over export control policy, particular economic interests lost out, repeatedly. The ability of central state actors, the executive in this instance, to prevail over domestic actors by changing or opposing the demands of such actors is one measure of their capacity. Stephen Krasner, *Defending the National Interest*, p. 6; Theda Skocpol, "Bringing the State Back In: Current Research," p. 7.

27. James G. March and Johan P. Olsen, "The New Institutionalism: Organizational Factors in Political Life," p. 742.

28. As Skocpol has noted, "[state actors] matter not simply because of the goal-oriented activities of state officials. They matter because their organizational configurations, along with their overall patterns of activity, affect political culture, encourage some kinds of group formation and collective actions (but not others) and make possible the raising of certain political issues (but not others)." Skocpol, "Bringing the State Back In," p. 21. The state may be viewed as the collection of individuals at the pinnacle of state power but, in addition, it "may be viewed as organizations through which official collectivities may pursue distinctive goals, realizing them more or less effectively given the available state resources in relation to social settings" (p. 28).

29. For example Bauer, Pool, and Dexter have suggested the importance of institutional and organizational factors in shaping policy outcomes: "The political outcome is something very different from the simple parallelogram of forces input by the conflicting groups. Summing up the conflicting interests at work is only the beginning of political analysis. The heart of political analysis is the discovery of the transformation process that make the political outputs something very different from what any of the interested parties wanted or sought." Bauer, Pool, and Dexter, *American Business and Public Policy*, pp. viii, ix.

30. As Theda Skocpol noted, Graham Allison's *Essence of Decision* and Morton Halperin's *Bureaucratic Politics and Foreign Policy* apply

the bureaucratic politics model to U.S. foreign policy by treating government agencies "as if they were pure analogues of the competing societal interest groups of classical pluralism. The structure and activities of the U.S. state as a whole receded from view and analysis in this approach." Skocpol, "Bringing the State Back In," p. 4.

31. This view is reflected in Woodrow Wilson's "The Study of Administration," in which he stated, "Administration lies outside the proper sphere of politics. Administrative questions are not political questions. Although politics sets the tasks for administrators, it should not be suffered to manipulate its offices" (p. 519). For modern discussions of the bureaucracy's neutral representational function, see Hannah Pitkin, *The Concept of Representation*, and David Rosenblom, "Forms of Bureaucratic Representation in the Federal Service."

32. Franz Schurmann's theory of U.S. imperialism posits a similar motivating force for what he views as America's imperial foreign economic policy. Schurmann envisions foreign policy as flowing from ideology. Ideology, for Schurmann, is grounded in the masses, and its demands are operationalized by the executive at the pinnacle of state power. The preconditions for empire include a strong realm of ideological "currents" that seek world peace, progress, and justice; a strong chief executive to personify and promulgate these currents; and military, political, and economic structures with global concerns.

Although in general agreement with some of Schurmann's discussion of the motivation for, albeit not his characterization of, America's postwar foreign policy, this book fundamentally disagrees with Schurmann's treatment of the bureaucracy. I suggest, at least with regard to U.S. export control policy, that the bureaucracy embodies as part of the executive the society's ideological, structural, and popular forces. Schurmann, in contrast, separates the bureaucracy from the executive and ideology and couples his understanding of foreign policy's origins with a model of bureaucratic, pluralistic politics. For Schurmann, the decisions that occasioned the post-1945 American empire were the result of the struggle between the "realm of ideology," as exemplified by the President and his office, and the "realm of interests," centered on the bureaucracy and representing a variety of particular interests. See Franz Schurmann, *The Logic of World Powers*.

33. Lowi noted the limitations that attend case studies of institutional dynamics: "At the end of an empirical study, neither approach [pluralist or elitist] affords a means for cumulating the data and findings in coherent and logical abstractions with other findings; they merely provide the basis for repeating the assumptions of the beginning." He concludes, "It seems to me that the reason for lack of interesting and non-obvious generalizations from cases and other specific empirical studies is clearly that the broad-gauged theories of politics

are not related, perhaps not relatable, to observable cases." Lowi, "American Business, Public Policy, Case Studies, and Political Theory," pp. 686–87.

34. See Allison and Szanton, *Remaking Foreign Policy*, pp. 68–69.

35. See, for example, Stephen D. Krasner, "Are Bureaucracies Important? Allison Wonderland."

36. Pastor, *Congress and the Politics of U.S. Foreign Economic Policy*, p. 35.

37. *Export Administration Act of 1979*, Pub. L. 96-72, 93 Stat. 503 (1979), later the *Export Administration Amendments Act of 1985*, Pub. L. 99-64.

38. A familiarity with legal and bureaucratic structures is necessary to understand U.S. foreign economic policy in general, and export control policy in particular. Historically, laws have been the means by which American society defined and circumscribed the reach of governmental authority in the economic realm. Law has been a particularly pervasive feature of U.S. trade policy. Although their view is perhaps overstated, Howell and Wolff in a trade law study maintained, "one is forced to conclude that to a degree unmatched in other nations, trade law is not merely an important aspect of U.S. trade policy—it actually is trade policy." Thomas R. Howell and Alan William Wolff, "The Role of Trade Law in the Making of Trade Policy," pp. 3–21.

39. Theda Skocpol has named these two characteristics "state autonomy" and "state capacity." By autonomy Skocpol means the ability of the state to formulate and pursue goals that are not merely reflections of the demands or interests of social groups, classes, or society. State capacity, in turn, refers to the ability of states "to implement official goals, especially over the actual or potential opposition of powerful social groups or in the face of recalcitrant socioeconomic circumstances." Skocpol, "Bringing the State Back In," p. 9.

40. For example, the Commerce Department publishes an annual report on U.S. export control administration and has done so for over 17 years.

2. The Origins of the U.S. Export Control System, 1949–1969

1. Even before World War II, the United States signaled its leadership in reducing trade barriers and trade discrimination with the passage of the Reciprocal Trade Agreements Act of 1934. During the war, the United States further pledged to eliminate trade barriers in the Lend-Lease Agreements, the Atlantic Charter, and the Bretton Woods Agreement.

2. Michael Mastanduno suggests that while the state and society were in general agreement with regard to East-West trade during the

1949–69 period, the state was more sensitive than Congress to the dissatisfaction of European allies with the U.S. strategic embargo policy directed at East European nations and the Soviet Union. As a result, Mastanduno points out, the state used a variety of policy instruments to permit the allies greater latitude in their export control policy than the hard-line strategic embargo advocated by Congress. See Michael Mastanduno, "The American State and East-West Trade Policy During the Hegemonic Period."

3. In an act dating from the First World War, the President had been empowered to control all exports to all destinations during time of war or, with the consent of Congress, during a national emergency under the Trading with the Enemy Act of 1917, and had been given limited authority to control the exportation of war materials before and during World War II under separate legislation. The Trading with the Enemy Act gives the President authority during time of war or during other period of international emergency declared by the President to prohibit, except under license, any kind of economic activity with designated countries. The President delegated administration of this act to the Secretary of the Treasury, who promulgated regulations through the Office of Foreign Assets Control.

The legislative purposes behind the Trading with the Enemy Act have been phrased in exceedingly general terms. Consequently, the statute has evolved over the years to serve a variety of domestic and international goals reflecting continuing interplay between the executive and Congress and a general increase in executive authority. The original purpose of the Trading with the Enemy Act of 1917 was to further the war effort by freezing Allied assets during World War I. The act originated in response to an international crisis and was not intended to apply to wholly domestic transactions, nor was it intended to be used during periods of "national emergency." Ironically, it was in response to the domestic banking crisis of 1933 that the President's authority under the Trading with the Enemy Act was revived and expanded to include the right to use the broad powers contained in the act to deal with a nonwartime national emergency.

By the close of World War II, the purpose of the Trading with the Enemy Act had grown from that of merely furthering war efforts. Despite the extraordinary powers it granted the President once he had declared a national emergency, Congress effectively provided no criteria limiting the emergencies a President could declare. In the cases mentioned in the text, Congress upheld the broad delegation of discretionary power over transactions involving the interests of designated foreign states or domestic institutions during periods of declared national emergency. As a result, this broad discretionary authority was used by the President after World War II to implement Treasury programs that supplemented the export control regime established by the

Export Control Act until that authority was supplanted by the International Emergency Economic Powers Act.

4. *An Act to Expedite the Strengthening of the National Defense*, ch. 703, 54 Stat. 712, 50 U.S.C.A. 701 (1940). The President controlled the export of steel scrap to Japan before World War II under the authority of this act. Presidential Proclamation 2417, July 2, 1940.

5. Act of June 30, 1942, ch. 636, sec. 6, 56 Stat. 463 (1942).

6. See S. Rept. 31, 81st Cong. 1st sess., 1949, describing the legislative background of the 1949 act: the act itself in Pub. L. 81-11, 63 Stat. 7 (1949), *as amended*, 50 U.S.C. app. secs. 2021–32 (1964) (terminated 1969). See also *Proposals for Reform of Export Controls for Advanced Technology* (Washington, D.C.: American Enterprise Institute, 1979), p. 4.

7. Report by the National Security Council, "Control of Exports to the U.S.S.R. and Eastern Europe," pp. 511–12.

8. "Memorandum of Conversation by the Acting Advisor to the Division of Occupied Areas Economic Affairs," pp. 524–26.

9. Exception was made for shipments to U.S. territories and most exports to Canada.

10. Senator Maybank in reporting out the Export Control Act of 1949 to the entire Senate summarized the purposes of the new legislation and noted that the new law was in keeping with the wishes of the executive branch: "Since the end of the war [export controls] have been used and at the present time they are being used, first to cushion the domestic economy from the inflationary effects of abnormal foreign demand for some of our supplies which are still short; second, to direct such goods as we can spare to those countries where need is greatest and where world recovery will be speeded up; and finally, to check exports of industrial commodities which might affect our national security.

"In other words, these controls are necessary now, and are being used, to protect the domestic economy by limiting exports of scarce materials, and to channel exports to countries where the need is greatest, and where our foreign policy and national security interests would be served best.

"President Truman, in his State of the Union Message, emphasized the need for continuation of these controls, and asked for renewal of the present legislation, together with provisions for more adequate enforcement." U.S., Congress, Senate, 81st Cong., 1st sess., February 7, 1949, *Congressional Record*, 95:949.

11. The Senate report accompanying the Act stated: "Export controls were retained after the war to reduce the inflationary effect of abnormal foreign demand upon our suppliers. Shortages were widespread, and unrestricted exports would have seriously aggravated the situation. We are still faced with shortages in important commodities,

mainly steel, the nonferrous metals, fibers, meats, fertilizers, certain chemicals and certain building materials, although the domestic and world supply situation has improved since the end of the war, particularly during the past year—the first year of the European recovery program." U.S., Congress, Senate, Senator Maybank in reporting out the Export Control Act of 1949, S. Rept. 31, 81st Cong., 1st sess., 1949.

12. U.S., Congress, Senate, 81st Cong., 1st sess., February 7, 1949, *Congressional Record*, 95:1368.

13. U.S., Congress, Senate, S. Rept. 1775, pt. 2, 80th Cong., 2d sess., 1948, p. 15.

14. U.S., Congress, Senate, S. Rept. 31, 81st Cong., 1st sess., 1949.

15. See Joseph Marion Jones, *The Fifteen Weeks* for a detailed discussion of this period.

16. On COCOM, see John R. McIntyre and Richard T. Cupitt, "East-West Strategic Trade Control: Crumbling Consensus."

17. In response to U.S. concerns regarding expanding trade between the Eastern bloc and Western Europe, President Truman sent Secretary of Commerce Averell Harriman to Europe in August 1948 to enlist allied cooperation in stemming the sale of goods and technology to "the U.S.S.R. and its satellites which ... would contribute to Soviet military potential"—a policy advocated by the U.S. National Security Council in December, 1947 and incorporated into Commerce Department regulations the following year. See Gary K. Bertsch, "Western Strategic Trade Controls: Goals, Policies, Politics, and the Future," p. 3.

18. U.S., Congress, House, H. Rept. 524, 91st Cong., 1st sess., 1969, p. 17. The asymmetrical agreement between the United States and its COCOM partners supports Arthur Stein's theory that a hegemon cannot act alone in establishing a trading regime but must use its resources to enlist cooperation through agreements with weaker states. See Arthur A. Stein, "The Hegemon's Dilemma: Great Britain, the United States, and the International Economic Order," p. 358.

19. U.S., Congress, House, H. Rept. 524, 91st Cong., 1st sess., 1969, p. 17.

20. The Export Control Act was subsequently renewed in 1956, 1958, 1960, and 1962. See Berman and Garson, "United States Export Controls," p. 799.

21. 22 U.S.C. secs. 1611 *et seq.* (1970).

22. *Ibid.*

23. *Ibid.*, secs. 1612–13.

24. For the current provisions see *International Security Assistance and Arms Export Control Act of 1976* (AECA), Pub. L.. 94-329, 90 Stat. 729, *U.S. Code*, vol. 22, secs. 2751–96C (1976 and Supp. IV 1980), as amended by the *International Security and Development Cooperation Act of 1981*, Pub. L. 97-13. The AECA establishes a system of licenses

for the registration of manufacturers, exporters, and importers of defense articles or services. The AECA also regulates manufacturing licenses and technical assistance agreements entered into between U.S. persons and foreign, private, or governmental entities relating to items on the U.S. Munitions List, including technical data.

25. 54 Stat. 712, 714 (1940).

26. Export control authority was given to the Economic Defense Board, Exec. Order 8900, 6 *Federal Register* 4795 (1941) (renamed the Board of Economic Warfare, Exec. Order 8982, 6 *Federal Register* 6530 [1941]); to the Office of Economic Warfare, Exec. Order 9361, 8 Federal Register 9861 (1943); to the Foreign Economic Administrator, Exec. Order 9380, 8 Federal Register 13081 (1943).

27. Exec. Order 9380, 10 Federal Register 12245 (1945); Department of Commerce Order 390, 10 Federal Register 13130 (1945).

28. John R. McIntyre has speculated as to the reasons for Commerce Department jurisdiction over export controls, suggesting that "the end of World War II and the return to a peacetime economy had a lot to do with it." He adds: "It is arguable that Commerce was chosen because it is much in the nature of an interlocking directorate" covering a great many functions and because "the control function did not readily fit anywhere else." John R. McIntyre, *Interagency Policy Implementation: The Case of U.S. Export Licensing of Advanced Technology.*

29. These new institutional responsibilities were not warmly received by the department. "Indeed, in 1949, Secretary of Commerce Sawyer frankly said of export control policy that 'it is a difficult and somewhat unpleasant task,' and that 'I would be very glad if some other department would take it all over.'" Berman and Garson, "United States Export Controls," pp. 805–6. Secretary Sawyer was, as a matter of principle, opposed to all governmental regulations or subsidies; interview with Dr. Thomas Blaisdell, former Assistant Secretary of Commerce under Secretary Sawyer, Washington, D.C., November 26, 1984.

30. Section 4(a) of the Export Control Act of 1949 (cited in note 6 above).

31. U.S. Congress, House, Select Committee on Export Controls, *Investigation and Study of the Administration, Operation, and Enforcement of the Export Control Act of 1949, and Related Acts*, 87th Cong., 1st sess., 1961, p. 87 (Statement of Secretary of State Dean Rusk).

32. John R. McIntyre, "East-West Technology Transfer Policy," p. 26. McIntyre describes export licensing policy as evolving along two polar extremes of economic warfare and pure free trade. Next along the continuum from economic warfare is "selective economic warfare," i.e., items should be restricted if they are either not already possessed by the Soviet Bloc or not available from other sources. Whenever there is a doubt as to the "strategic" quality of a good, the tendency is to

deny its export and to err on the side of caution. This is the policy that still dominates export licensing today, despite its rejection by Congress in the 1979 Export Administration Act. McIntyre trenchantly notes that selective economic warfare naturally is the policy choice for a President who desires to preserve maximum flexibility in his dealings with the Soviet Union.

Another policy type is termed "qualified free trade." This approach recognizes that certain highly advanced technologies should be restricted on purely strategic grounds, but that few such goods exist in the context of today's interdependent world economy. Finally, the "free trade" model holds that, short of outright military conflicts, trade should rarely if ever be used to achieve strategic, foreign policy, or military goals. *Ibid.*, pp. 27–28.

33. *Ibid.*

34. Judith Goldstein has discussed the importance of institutional mandates. Her study of U.S. import policy demonstrates how the Great Depression discredited protectionism in the 1930s and 1940s and contributed mightily to the enduring liberal ideology of U.S. trade institutions. See Judith L. Goldstein, "The Political Economy of Trade: Institutions of Protection."

35. No special certification is required from the Department of Commerce to engage in export-import trade. However, exports must be authorized by either a general or a validated license. A general license is an authorization published in the Regulations that permits exports without requiring the exporter to submit a license application. A validated license is a formal authorization document issued by the Commerce Department's Office of Export Control after it reviews a written license application submitted by the exporter. An individual validated license permits an exporter to ship a specified commodity or technology to a named consignee in a particular country for a designated use.

36. Historically, the Office of Export Control had a Policy Planning Division charged with developing overall policies and procedures for the licensing of exports. Nonetheless, a study by the General Accounting Office (GAO) found that the planning and policy guidance function was neglected in favor of resolving disputes and coordinating relations with other export control agencies. The GAO concluded that the work of the Policy Planning Division was devoted to resolving interagency differences on a case-by-case basis rather than developing policies which incorporate technological advances and changes in East-West relations into the list of controlled goods and destinations. U.S. General Accounting Office, *The Government's Role in East-West Trade: Problems and Issues*, p. 30.

37. See Baldwin, *Economic Statecraft*, pp. 222–23.

38. During its history, at least two levels of interagency reviews were available to consider those matters which the Operating Commit-

tee could not resolve. ACEP, the Advisory Committee on Export Policy, composed of political appointees, and the Cabinet-level EARB, Export Administration Review Board, sat atop the Operating Committee. These review committees were composed of representatives from the Commerce Department and consulted agencies and rendered decisions based on unanimous consent. Ultimately, matters not resolved by the EARB were referred to the President for a final decision.

39. In 1949, Commerce Department Secretary Sawyer noted that the Office of Export Control was handling so many license applications that its funds ran out within a year.

The office handled more than 10,000 applications per week in 1949 with only 125 personnel. U.S. Congress, Senate, Subcommittee of the Committee on Banking and Currency, *Extension of Export Controls*, 81st Congress, 1st sess., 1949, p. 1.

40. Bruce W. Jentleson, "From Consensus to Conflict: The Domestic Political Economy of East-West Energy Trade Policy" (quoting from *Congressional Record*, February 17, 1949).

41. *Ibid.*, n. 22.

42. See Holbert N. Carroll, *The House of Representatives and Foreign Affairs*, pp. 59–64.

43. In 1948, 7 out of 10 Americans surveyed believed that East-West trade should be discontinued. Gunnar Adler-Karlsson, *Western Economic Warfare, 1947–1967*.

44. U.S., Congress, Senate, Committee on Banking and Currency, *Extension of Export Controls Hearings*, 81st Cong., 1st sess., 1949, p. 70 [hereafter Senate Hearings 1949].

45. *Ibid.*, p. 170.

46. U.S., Congress, House, Committee on Banking and Currency, *Export Control Act of 1949 Hearings*, 81st Cong., 1st sess., 1949, p. 171.

47. Senate Hearings 1949, p. 186.

48. See U.S., Congress, Senate, Committee on Government Operations, *East-West Trade*, 84th Cong., 2d sess., 1956; *Statements of Industry Officials, Hearings Before a Subcommittee on Investigations*, 84th Cong., 2d sess., 1956.

49. Senate Hearing 1949, p. 176. Sinclair, when speaking to this issue, noted a similar complaint: "Generally speaking, the Office of International Trade has done a good job in removing commodities from individual licensing requirements as soon as the domestic supply situation warranted. Other departments, however, including Agriculture and State, have not evidenced the same interest in reducing the scope of export controls. Both from this standpoint and as a check on efficient administration in the Office of International Trade, the Congress has a very definite task which certainly should be reviewed at least once a year. This is especially desirable in view of the broad

NOTES: ORIGINS OF THE SYSTEM

powers given to the Office of International Trade under the last sentence of section 4(b) of S. 548." *Ibid.*, p. 186.

50. See U.S. Congress, Senate, S. Rept. 1775, pt. 2, 80th Congress, 2d sess., 1948, p. 96.

51. Berman and Garson, "United States Export Controls," p. 800.

52. See U.S., Congress, House, *Investigation and Study of the Administration, Operation, and Enforcement of the Export Control Act of 1949, and Related Acts,* 87th Cong., 1st sess., 1961.

53. See, for example, U.S. Congress, House, 87th Cong., 2d sess., February 1, 1962, *Congressional Record,* 108:1400.

54. 50 U.S.C. app. sec. 2021(b) (1964).

55. Pub. L 87-515, 76 Stat. 127 (1962); 50 U.S.C. app. sec. 2023(a) (1964), *as amended* (Supp. I, 1965).

56. The 1962 amendment explicitly provides that it is the policy of the United States "to use its economic resources and advantages in trade with Communist-dominated nations to further the national security and foreign policy objectives of the United States." 50 U.S.C. app. sec. 2022 (1964), *as amended* (Supp. I, 1965).

The Department of Commerce, the executive agency with primary responsibility for the implementation of export controls under the Export Control Act, interpreted this amendment in the following way: "Having in mind that the economic resources and advantages in trade possessed by the United States obviously include much more than the power to impose export controls, the Department construes the scope of this amendment as transcending the preexisting statutory authority and responsibility invested in the Department under the act. . . . [T]he Department construes this amendment providing congressional policy authorization to vary the scope and severity of export control to particular countries, from time to time, as national security and foreign policy interests require. . . ." *Export Control,* 61st Quarterly Report (1962), p. 5.

57. U.S., Congress, Senate, S. Rept. 1576, 87th Cong., 2d sess., 1962, p. 1817.

58. U.S., Department of State, *The Battle Act in New Times: Fifteenth Report to Congress* (1961), p. 5.

59. Mastanduno, "The American State and East-West Trade Policy During the Hegemonic Period," pp. 25–34.

60. The difference between the 1960s and 1970s was not so much who controlled policy but the ends that policy served. In the 1960s the President possessed a somewhat greater interest than the congressional majority did in expanding East-West trade. By 1969, it was Congress that was out in front on East-West trade liberalization. This transition is discussed in chapter 3.

61. Jentleson, "East-West Energy Trade," p. 637.

62. Mastanduno, "The American State and East-West Trade Policy During the Hegemonic Period," p. 28.
63. Interview data, Washington, D.C., November 18, 1985.
64. Mastanduno, "The American State and East-West Trade Policy During the Hegemonic Period," pp. 28–29.
65. See U.S. Department of State, *The Battle Act in New Times*, pp. 67–69.
66. See Remarks of President Johnson at Doylestown, Pa., October 16, 1966, 2 Weekly Comp. Pres. Docs. 1512, 1514 (1966) implemented by the Department of Commerce, 31 *Federal Register* 13,699 (1966).

3. U.S. Export Control Law and Policy in the 1970s

1. U.S., Congress, Senate, Committee on Banking and Currency, *Export Expansion and Regulation*, 91st Cong., 1st sess., 1969.
2. Krasner, *Defending the National Interest*, p. 12.
3. *Export Administration Act of 1969*, Pub. L. 91-184, 83 Stat. 841, 50 U.S.C. app., secs. 2401(2), 2402(1) (B) (1969).
4. ". . . Much has happened since 1949. The Soviet Union has rebuilt its economy so that its technological and industrial level is greater than ever. Thus it can now produce many products which it formerly might have sought from the United States. . . . By withholding trade, we encourage a nation to develop its own resources. Rigid export restrictions result in a denial forcing the creation of new industrial capacity to produce the item denied." U.S., Congress, Senate, Committee on Banking and Currency, *Export Expansion and Regulation*, 91st Cong., 1st sess., 1969 (hereafter Senate Hearings 1969), pp. 2, 4 (remarks of Senator Edmund Muskie [D-Me.]).
5. This assertion that Congress, in general, was responding to changes in the domestic and international environment is not meant to ignore the fact that congressmen, in particular, were responding to specific demands of their constituents. It is no accident that Senator Mondale, who spearheaded efforts in the Senate to liberalize export controls, hails from a state with high technology and agricultural interests—the United States' chief export commodities at the time in question.
6. U.S., Congress, House, *Export Control Act Extension*, H. Rept. 524, 91st Cong., 1st sess., 1969, p. 10.
7. For example, Senator Muskie noted that "American businessmen complain that licensing delays and red tape lose sales in Eastern Europe and often prevent American businesses from trying to develop the market. If goods equivalent to American products are available elsewhere, other countries will buy from the alternative sources to avoid the complicated paperwork and restrictions imposed by the American

Government, which also result in long delays in delivery to customers who can find faster and less complicated arrangements by dealing with other western countries." Senate Hearings 1969, p. 5 (remarks of Senator Muskie).

8. U.S., Congress, House, Committee on Banking and Currency, *Hearings before the Subcommittee on International Trade to Extend and Amend the Export Act of 1949*, 91st Cong., 1st sess., 1969 (hereafter House Hearings 1969), p. 9.

9. Senate Hearings 1969, p. 9.

10. U.S., Congress, Senate, *Export Expansion and Regulation Act*, S. Rept. 336, 91st Cong., 1st sess., 1969, p. 4.

11. *Ibid.*, p. 11.

12. *Ibid.*

13. "The proposal that would replace the present Export Control Act is based on the assertion that factors which brought about the enactment of the Export Control Act no longer exist. We cannot agree with such an assertion. It is suggested that we are now living in an era in which the Soviet Union presents a reduced threat to the security of the United States. We find no evidence that such a new era had been ushered in. In fact, we consider the Soviet Union as a much greater threat to the security of the United States than it was when the Export Control Act of 1949 was passed." *Ibid.*, pp. 22 (statement of Senators Wallace F. Bennett and John G. Tower).

14. 50 U.S.C. app. sec. 2402 (Cum. Supp. 1978).

The attempt to balance the possibly conflicting goals of national security and free trade in the Export Administration Act of 1969 was reflected in the following findings set forth in the opening section of the Act:

(1) The quantity and composition of United States exports may affect both the domestic economy and United States foreign policy.

(2) Unrestricted exports "may make a significant contribution to the military potential of any nation or . . . adversely affect [United States] national security. . . ."

(3) The "unwarranted restriction of exports . . . has a serious adverse effect on our balance of payments, particularly when export restrictions applied by the United States are more extensive than export restrictions imposed by countries with which the United States had defense treaty commitments."

(4) "The uncertainty of policy towards certain categories of exports has curtailed the efforts of American business in those categories to the detriment of the overall attempt to improve the trade balance of the United States."

(5) Unreasonable restrictions on access to world supplies can cause worldwide political and economic instability, interfere with free

international trade, and retard the growth and development of nations.
Ibid., sec. 2401(1)–(5).
15. *Ibid.*
16. *Export Control Act of 1949*, Pub. L. 81-11, 63 Stat. 7, sec. 4(a)(2)(6) (1949).
17. *Ibid.*
18. *Export Administration Act of 1969*, Pub. L. 91-184, 83 Stat. 841, sec. 4(a)(2) (1969). The statute required the publication of regulations and the establishment of an office in the Department of Commerce to gather evidence on foreign availability.
19. *Ibid.*, sec. 4(a)(1).
20. Henry Kissinger, *The White House Years*, p. 154.
21. S. 813, 91st Cong., 1st sess. (1969); H.R. 4293, 91st Cong., 1st sess. (1969).
22. Senate Hearings 1969, p. 273.
23. Interview data, November and December 1985.
24. *Ibid.* Raymond Garthoff described the executive's autonomous interest in export control at that time: "Many leading liberals, and conservative business interests as well, argued for removing 'remnants of the cold war' from this basic trade legislation. . . . Nixon and Kissinger, on the other hand, saw normalization of trade relations with the Soviet Union as a card they could play; as Kissinger later put it expanding trade without a political quid pro quo was a gift; there was very little the Soviet Union could do for us economically. It did not seem to me unreasonable to require Soviet restraint in such trouble spots as the Middle East, Berlin and Southeast Asia in return." Raymond L. Garthoff, *Détente and Confrontation: American-Soviet Relations from Nixon to Reagan*, pp. 90–91.
25. Senate Hearings 1969, p. 270.
26. *Ibid.*, p. 272.
27. House Hearings 1969, p. 118.
28. *Ibid.*, pp. 118, 119.
29. *Ibid.*, p. 123.
30. Senate Hearings 1969, pp. 274–75, 286.
31. The Commerce Department expressed its understanding of the importance of foreign availability assessment: "It is clear that the industrial capacity and capability of other free world nations has been increasing and, as U.S. companies have established operations overseas, there has been a growing availability abroad of the advanced technology and products which are sought by the Eastern Europeans. We are increasingly taking this factor into consideration in the determination of whether export approval would in fact prove detrimental to the national security of the United States. This is part of our practice today." House Hearings 1969, p. 122.

The Defense Department made a similar claim that reflects the executive's narrow reading of its responsibility to assess foreign availability of controlled commodities: "In the course of revising the commodity control list, we constantly take into account the availability elsewhere in the non-Communist world of commodities with strategic significance. We also take into account known advances in Communist technology. It often happens that what seemed to be comparable goods in other parts of the free world turn out not to be when the details of availability, quality, delivery rates, reliability, service support, and relative costs are more closely scrutinized. When it can be shown that such goods are indeed comparable and readily obtainable elsewhere, our export control list is revised accordingly." *Ibid.*, p. 119.

32. *Ibid.*, p. 128.
33. *Ibid.*, p. 119.
34. *Ibid.*, p. 121.
35. *Ibid.*, p. 116.
36. See Senate Hearings 1969, p. 285.
37. "Trade Curbs Eased, President Retains Final Veto on Sales," *National Journal*, January 3, 1970, pp. 9–11. Similarly, Harold J. Berman, special counsel to the Senate Banking and Currency Committee, described the act as "mood" legislation and conceded: "If the Executive wishes to read the Act in its narrowest and most literal sense, there will be no need for it to do much other than what it has done under the pre-existing law, except to make various reports to Congress. If, however, the Executive reads the Act according to its spirit, and not merely according to its letter, there may be substantial changes. . . ." Harold J. Berman, "The Export Administration Act of 1969: Analysis and Appraisal," p. 27.
38. James L. Sundquist, "Congress and the President: Enemies or Partners?" in Henry Owens and Charles L. Schultze, eds., *Setting National Priorities: The Next Ten Years*, pp. 583–618.
39. Harold Berman, a contemporary observer, identified administration opposition as the chief reason the 1969 act was not binding on the executive, adding: "It was the Senate Banking and Currency Committee, especially Senators Mondale and Muskie, with valuable support from Senators Brooke and Perry, together with some others, which undertook the task of initiating legislation against the opposition of the Administration." Berman, "The Export Administration Act of 1969," p. 27.
40. U.S. Congress, Senate, Senator Jackson speaking for the Amendment to the Trade Act of 1974, 92d Cong., 2d sess., 1972, *Congressional Record* 118:33658.
41. See Paula Stern, *The Water's Edge: Domestic Politics and the Making of American Foreign Policy* for a detailed discussion of the passage of the Jackson-Vanik amendment.

42. Mastanduno, "The American State and East-West Trade Policy During the Hegemonic Period."
43. Graham T. Allison, "Overview of Finding and Recommendations from Defense and Arms Control Cases," p. 21.
44. See U.S., Congress, Senate, Committee on Banking, Housing, and Urban Affairs, *Equal Export Opportunity Act and the International Economic Policy Act of 1972*, S. Rept. 890, 92d Cong., 2d sess., June 19, 1972, pp. 1–4.
45. *Ibid.*
46. According to Commerce Department figures, 64.6 percent of the items completely removed from the Commodity Control List (CCL) and 50.74 percent of the items completely or partially removed from the CCL for export to Communist destinations during the 1970 to mid-1973 period were decontrolled in the final quarter of 1972 and the first two quarters of 1973. U.S., Department of Commerce, *Export Control Quarterly Report* (Washington: GPO, 1970–73).
47. U.S., Department of Commerce, *Special Report to the President and the Congress*, May 29, 1973. Certain entries contain hundreds of actual commodities. See, for example, Commodity Control List entry 4707B, "Synthetic organic agricultural chemicals."
48. According to one source who both designed the policy and later implemented it, President Nixon and NSC Director Kissinger sensed the importance of using American trade and technology against the Soviets, and when the executive realized that Congress was going ahead with new legislation, the executive made a conscious decision to implement the new legislation slowly and only in exchange for political concessions by the Soviet Union.
49. A similar situation existed with regard to circuit boards and other computer subassemblies, despite the rapid obsolescence in computer technology.

The 1979 Export Administration Act attempted to rectify this situation by requiring the "indexing" of export controls, i.e., the upward adjustment of performance specifications in control entries to reflect technological progress. Executive institutions did not implement this legislative initiative, however. In 1981, the General Accounting Office reported that indexation was not being implemented. With few exceptions, indexation, to date, has not become an institutional feature of national security export licensing. See U.S., Congress, Comptroller General, *Export Control Regulation Could Be Reduced Without Affecting National Security* (May 26, 1982), p. 6.

50. Congress explicitly strengthened its call for improved foreign availability assessment in the 1972 and 1977 amendments to the 1969 act. See *Export Administration Act of 1969 as Amended by the Equal Export Opportunity Act of 1972*, Pub. L 92-412, 86 Stat. 644, sec. 4(b)(2)(B)

(1972); *Export Administration Amendments of 1977*, 95th Cong. 1st sess., 1977, p. 9.

51. An exhaustive analysis of export control administration by the General Accounting Office concluded: "Simply put, no single person was in charge of managing the foreign availability analysis. The task groups [of various executive agencies] dealt with the intelligence agencies on differing bases and there was some apparent breakdown in the use of the information that was available." U.S., Congress, Comptroller General, *Export Controls: Need to Clarify and Simplify Administration, Report to the Congress by the Comptroller General of the United States* (March 1, 1979), p. 29.

Similarly, the Office of Technology Assessment's report on technology and East-West trade noted that by 1979 there had been no fundamental change in this aspect of U.S. licensing and listed examples of the bureaucracy's failure to consider technical developments both within and outside COCOM. U.S., Congress, Office of Technology Assessment, *Technology and East-West Trade* (1979), p. 142.

52. See 50 *Federal Register* 10503 (March 19, 1985).

53. A comparison of authorized funding and staff levels at the Office of Export Administration in the 1970s reveals that funding and personnel were severely cut in 1973 and 1974, corresponding to the decontrol of many commodities and a consequent reduction in the number of export license applications received by the OEA at this time. In the next five years, however, the number of authorized personnel increased 18 percent, while the number of licenses processed rose 27 percent.

As for decentralization, the Defense Department was consulted on national security export controls to the Eastern bloc. The Departments of State and Energy and, to a lesser extent, the National Aeronautics and Space Administration were the other principal consultants. The Central Intelligence Agency serves in an advisory capacity, as do other agencies when their expertise is pertinent. Decisions on contentious license applications are made only after the consulted agencies unanimously consent. If unanimous approval is not secured directly, the disagreement is resolved through a negotiation within a series of multiagency committees composed of representatives at the Assistant Secretary level known as ACEP, the Advisory Committee on Export Policy, where a rule of unanimity also governs decisions. If any interagency dispute remains, the matter is addressed by the Export Administration Review Board, consisting of the Secretaries of Commerce, State, and Defense, with final authority residing in the President.

54. Congress addressed the issue of licensing delays again in 1974, 1977, and 1979; the topic is discussed in detail in chapter 4.

On the attitude of exporters, see U.S., Congress, Comptroller General, *Administration of U.S. Export Licensing Should Be Consolidated to*

Be More Responsive to Industry, Report to the Congress by the Comptroller General of the United States, October 31, 1978.

55. U.S., Congress, House, *International Economic Policy Act of 1972,* H. Rept. 1260, 92d Cong., 2d sess., 1972, p. 4.

56. *Equal Export Opportunity Act,* Pub. L 92-412, 86 Stat. 644, sec. 103 (1972).

57. *Ibid.,* sec. 105.

58. *Export Administration Act of 1974,* Pub. L. 93-500, 88 Stat. 1552 (1974).

59. *Export Administration Act of 1969,* Pub. L. 91-184, 83 Stat. 841, sec. 5(a) (1969).

60. An example of business frustration with the failure to translate its participation in TACs into meaningful policy reforms was expressed in a statement submitted by the Western Electrical Manufacturers Association to the Senate Committee on Banking, Housing, and Urban Affairs: "For example, the Technical Advisory Committee on Computers worked with the National Bureau of Standards for over a year to improve the technical criteria required to more effectively measure computer performance. It appears that the new standards were rejected and, despite all the work, the same old obsolete criteria will continue to be used. It is unfortunate that this happened, but more disturbing is the fact that this Technical Advisory Committee has not received any reasons why its recommendations were unacceptable. In situations like these, questions about the meaningfulness of the role of the Technical Advisory Committees are bound to occur." U.S., Congress, House, Committee on International Relations, *Extension of the Export Administration Act of 1969,* 95th Cong., 1st sess., 1977, p. 601.

61. U.S., Congress, Comptroller General, *Administration of U.S. Export Licensing Should Be Consolidated to Be More Responsive to Industry,* October 31, 1978.

62. The General Accounting Office (GAO) compiled 119 licensing histories, including 68 applications that took 90 or more days to approve and 51 applications that were denied for national security and foreign policy reasons. On the basis of those licensing histories and interviews with officials of the licensing community and with exporters, the GAO reached its conclusions. *Ibid.*

63. *Ibid.,* p. 33.

64. *Ibid.*

65. U.S., Congress, Senate, S. Rept. 890, 92d Cong., 2d sess., 1972, p. 3.

66. John R. McIntyre and Richard T. Cupitt, "East-West Strategic Trade Control: Crumbling Consensus," pp. 90–91. By a second estimate, as of June 1, 1979, COCOM multilateral controls numbered 126 entries, and unilateral U.S. controls extended over 72 additional en-

tries. See Kenneth W. Abbott, "Linking Trade to Political Goals: Foreign Policy Export Controls in the 1970s and 1980s," p. 759, n. 105.

There are limits to the meaningfulness of comparing the number of commodity categories on the U.S. unilateral list with the COCOM list. For example, the final two commodity categories on the U.S. list are "basket" entries for chemicals which encompass dozens of actual commodities. In general, the results with regard to harmonizing U.S. policy with that of COCOM during the 1970s were mixed; unilateral controls were lifted on a variety of commodities, but no reduction in technology controls was implemented by the United States.

67. U.S., Congress, Comptroller General, *Export Controls: Need to Clarify Policy and Simplify Administration, Report to the Congress by the Comptroller General,* 1979, p. iii.

68. Bertsch, "Western Strategic Trade Controls." A study of U.S. export controls conducted by Rand reached a similar conclusion: "all requests for [COCOM embargo] list tightening and most resistance to list loosening came from the United States, and on all the exceptions requests in COCOM history that were allowed, the United States voted yes only once." Robert A. Klitgaard, *National Security and Export Controls,* p. 15.

69. Two specific disputes between the United States and France in the mid-1970s illustrate the problem of differing interpretation of licensing standards. In the first case, the French government authorized a French manufacturer to export stretch forming presses (which can be used for manufacturing airplane frames) to the Soviet Union despite protests from the U.S. government concerning its more restrictive reading of the COCOM controls governing this commodity. In the second case, the United States strenuously objected to a French sale of semiconductor technology to Poland. Moreover, there were times when COCOM countries simply chose to ignore the multilateral process entirely.

COCOM has no enforcement powers per se. It does have a subcommittee which develops coordinated procedures to deter violations and which exchanges information on national enforcement.

70. In general, tensions arising from differing interests within COCOM were also vented through requests for exceptions. Exceptions, which must be approved unanimously by COCOM, permit the export of an item to a controlled destination if the security risk is acceptable. By 1978, exception requests had increased to about 1,000 annually, valued at slightly more than $200 million. The United States submitted about one-half of these requests, raising questions within COCOM as to the sincerity of stricter U.S. licensing policies. The majority of these requests were approved, either initially or after revisions. While the number of exception requests increased during the 1970s, the value

of COCOM exception cases continued to represent less than 1 percent of the value of total exports from COCOM countries to controlled destinations. The exception process was both an outlet for differences in licensing processes and a point of contention between COCOM countries. Delays in reaching exception decisions, especially by the United States, have been another source of friction.

71. EDAC is chaired by the Assistant Secretary of State for Economic and Business Affairs. This interagency committee consists of representatives from the State, Defense, and Commerce Departments and from the Nuclear Regulatory Commission and the Central Intelligence Agency.

72. U.S., Congress, House, Committee on International Relations, *Extension of the Export Administration Act of 1969*, 95th Cong., 1st sess., 1977, p. 310.

73. *Report of the President's Task Force to Improve Export Administration Licensing Procedures* (Draft), September 22, 1976, p. 112.

74. See U.S., Congress, Senate, S. Rept. 890, 92d Cong., 2d sess., 1972, p. 4. Discussions with EDAC's participants during the 1970s suggest that all these criticisms were justified.

75. U.S., Congress, House, Committee on Banking and Currency, *Extension of the Export Administration Act of 1969*, 92d Cong., 2d sess., 1972, p. 321.

76. In describing the Export Control Act, Berman and Garson stated: "Probably no single piece of legislation gives more power to the President to control American commerce. Subject only to the vaguest standards of 'foreign policy' and 'national security and welfare,' he has authority to cut off the entire export trade of the United States, or any part of it, or to deny 'export privileges' to any and all persons." Berman and Garson, "United States Export Controls," p. 792.

4. *Institutional Influence on Licensing: The Reforms of 1974, 1977, and 1979*

1. Joan Edelman Spero in her discussion of this period noted the words of then Treasury Secretary Michael Blumenthal: "Experience indicates that attempts to use economic pressure to achieve noneconomic concessions are likely to be ineffective." Joan Edelman Spero, *The Politics of International Economic Relations*, p. 375.

2. U.S., President, "United States Export Policy," *Weekly Compilation of Presidential Documents* (September 1978), vol. 14, no. 39, p. 1633.

3. U.S., Congress, House, H. Rept. 190, 95th Cong., 1st sess., 1977, p. 12.

4. U.S. Congress, Office of Technology Assessment, *Technology and East-West Trade*, p. 139.

5. Those standards included responses to exporter applicants within specific time frames, as follows:
  (1) If a decision for final approval or disapproval of an application has not been made within 90 days, the applicant for an export license is to be notified in writing of the "specific circumstances requiring ... additional time and the estimated date when the decision will be made."
  (2) If a decision has not been made within 90 days, the applicant shall, to "the maximum extent consistent with the national security of the United States," be notified in writing of "questions raised and negative considerations or recommendations made by an agency ... and shall be accorded an opportunity to respond to such questions ... in writing ..." before a final decision. The Government "shall take fully into account the applicant's response...."
  (3) If an application is referred by the Department of Commerce to another agency, the Government shall provide, upon the applicants's request, "any documentation to be submitted ... in order to determine whether such documentation accurately describes the proposed export."
  (4) If an application is denied, the applicant "shall be informed in writing of the specific statutory basis for such denial."

Export Administration Amendments of 1977, Pub. L. 95-52, 91 Stat. 235, sec. 106 (1977).

6. *Export Administration Act of 1979*, Pub. L 96-72, 93 Stat. 503, sec. 10(b) (1979).

7. Studies have attempted to estimate the cost of export controls in dollars to U.S. industry and, in particular, the impact on high-technology industries. Although the lost sales are substantial, the primary cost of controls to U.S. industry is not the result of export controls placed on trade with the Soviet bloc. This trade has never been a major component of overall U.S. trade. Rather, the principal impact of controls falls on exports to noncommunist countries; controls on such exports are directed at preventing the subsequent diversion of U.S. exports to Communist destinations. By one estimate, in 1984 more than one-half of the projected $26 billion in total U.S. electronics exports, most of which were destined for Western Europe, were subject to costly requirements to secure specific government export authorization. National Academy of Sciences and National Academy of Engineering, *Briefing: Export Controls*.

Moreover, many of these exports are subject to commercially damaging delay.

8. The effects and importance of license processing delays to Ameri-

can exporters were reflected in a response to a congressional inquiry by Joseph E. Karth, President and General Manager, American League for Exports and Security Assistance, Inc., in which he stated that the United States was seen increasingly as an unreliable supplier of high-technology goods and services because of its complex licensing procedures and changing export policies. It was his belief that, as a consequence, nations simply do not seek these items from the United States, but buy them elsewhere. U.S., Congress, House, Committee on International Relations, *Hearings on Extension and Revision of the Export Administration Act of 1969*, (hereafter referred to as House Hearings 1977), 95th Cong., 1st sess., 1977, p. 958.

9. *Ibid.*

10. *Ibid.*, p. 960.

11. *Ibid.*, p. 969. Gray offered the following specific evidence of the effect of export controls on the export performance of American machine tool manufacturers: "In February of 1978, NMTBA conducted a survey of its members on the question of export licensing difficulties. Of the 90 respondents to the questionnaire, 30 export licensable machine tools to the Socialist countries, and another 9 companies have ceased attempts to do so because of past or anticipated difficulties in obtaining a license. Only 12 of these 39 companies indicated that they have never experienced licensing problems. The balance have experienced denials and/or delays. The estimated additional annual volume these companies claim they would receive, if it were not for unreasonable delays and/or licensing denials, exceeds by $10 million our industry's total shipments to the Socialist countries ($48 million) in 1977." *Ibid.*, p. 964.

12. *Ibid.*, p. 961. A report of the Comptroller General offered the following evidence of delays: "The Office of Export Administration issued 50,737 licenses in 1977. It denied 348, and 1,291 applications took 90 or more days to be approved. While the total number of applications increased by 5 percent in 1977 over 1976, the number of applications taking more than (1) 30 days to process increased by 47 percent, (2) 90 days to process increased by 52 percent, and (3) 180 days to process increased by 50 percent.

"The GAO's random survey of applications which took 90 days or more to issue licenses revealed that the average decisionmaking time for 68 applications was 228 days. Even after discounting 18 of these applications that were delayed because of a foreign policy embargo, the average decisionmaking time for the 50 applications was 198 days." U.S., Comptroller General, *Administration of U.S. Export Licensing Should Be Consolidated to Be More Responsive to Industry*, Report to the Congress by the Comptroller General, October 31, 1978, pp. i, ii, 22–23.

13. See House Hearings 1977, pp. 518–20.

14. "Any system which clarifies and simplifies the present system is

desirable. The establishment of clear suspense points is a step in the right direction. These time limits must be closely monitored to ensure that difficult cases are not arbitrarily denied by the bureaucracy as a safe way of meeting these time limits." U.S., Congress, House, Subcommittee on International Economic Policy and Trade, Committee on Foreign Affairs, *Extension and Revision of the Export Administration Act of 1969*, 96th Cong., 1st sess., 1979, p. 206.

15. *Ibid.*, p. 620 (statement of Frank A. Weill, Assistant Secretary for Industry and Trade, Department of Commerce).

16. *Ibid.*, p. 678.

17. *Ibid.*, p. 620.

18. U.S., Congress, Office of Technology Assessment, *Technology and East-West Trade 1979*, p. 139.

19. House Hearings 1977, p. 505 (statement of Thomas Christiansen, Manager of International Trade Relations, Hewlett-Packard, representing the American Electronics Association).

20. *Ibid.*, pp. 515–17. For example, 30 percent of Hewlett-Packard's 1,130 applications during the period of July 1, 1976 to December 31, 1976 required more than 90 days to process. This figure declined to only 27 percent for 428 applications processed during 1978.

21. U.S., Congress, House, Committee on Foreign Affairs, *Export Administration Amendments Act of 1981*, 97th Cong., 1st sess., 1981, p. 95.

22. U.S., Congress, House, Committee on Foreign Affairs, 98th Cong., 1st sess., March 1, 1983. Prepared Statement of Lionel H. Olmer, Under Secretary for Trade Administration, Department of Commerce, Before the Subcommittee on International Economic Policy and Trade, U.S. House of Representatives, Washington, D.C., March 1, 1983, mimeo, p. 15.

23. For example, the Department of Defense or its consulted agencies would often delay its recommendation on a license because it opposed exporting to a Communist country a good or technology and lacked clear and sufficient grounds to deny the application. Similarly, delays were used by the State Department to avoid denying a license application until sufficient political pressure for its approval could be arranged. Interview data.

24. "The fundamental criterion employed by the Department of Defense in making licensing recommendations is whether the export of the goods or technology being considered will significantly increase the military capability of a controlled country." U.S., Congress, Senate, Committee on Banking, Housing, and Urban Affairs, *Hearings on the Extension of the Export Administration Act*, 94th Cong., 2d sess., 1976, p. 153 (statement of Roger E. Shields, Deputy Assistant Secretary, International Economic Affairs, Department of Defense). While alleging that the Defense Department "is not opposed to peaceful trade

nor to the expansion of commercial and economic ties with countries in the communist world," the Defense Department believed it should err on the side of restriction because the loss to the U.S. economy from a license denial, whatever the impact on the prospective vendor, could not be very great. "If on the other hand, [the Department] should err on the side of relaxing controls in a way which would enhance Soviet strategic capabilities, the price in subsequent increased defense costs and greater security risks could be very large." *Ibid.*, p. 164.

25. In the mid-1970s, the department believed its role was "to insure that the decisions made in the committee are consistent with the overall foreign policy objectives of the United States and with the U.S. position in the international community." U.S., Congress, Senate, Committee on Banking, Housing, and Urban Affairs, *Hearings on Extension of the Export Administration Act*, 94th Cong., 2d sess., 1976, p. 173 (statement of Maynard W. Glitman, Deputy Assistant Secretary, International Trade Policy, Department of State).

26. The Commerce Department explained its export licensing philosophy in the following manner: "The licensing considerations are focused primarily on national security, but such factors as foreign availability and economic benefit are not overlooked ... we concentrate first on the less flexible factor, the impact on U.S. national security. Economic and foreign policy factors take on increasing importance as strategic factors diminish." U.S., Congress, Senate, Committee on Banking, Housing, and Urban Affairs, *Hearings on the Extension of the Export Administration Act*, 94th Cong., 2d sess., 1976, p. 140 (statement of Arthur T. Downey, Deputy Assistant Secretary of Commerce for East-West Trade).

27. Despite some major differences in the 1980s between the Defense and Commerce Departments over export control policy, it should not be assumed that serious interagency differences were insurmountable —only that they were often time-consuming. For example, during the first six months of 1976, the Policy Planning Division of the Commerce Department's Office of Export Administration prepared approximately 12,000 memoranda summarizing licensing cases and forwarded them to the Department of Defense for its concurrence or recommendation. Of the approximately 12,000 memoranda, the Defense Department recommended denial of only 9 applications that Commerce had favored.

28. Baldwin, *Economic Statecraft*, pp. 222–23.

29. For example, Baldwin has criticized export licensing decision-making as based on the false premise that certain goods with possible military uses are inherently "strategic" and therefore must be controlled. As an alternative, Baldwin suggests that "a 'strategic' item is anything that is needed to pursue a given strategy that is relatively inefficient to produce at home." Consequently, trade restraints should

be based on a doctrine of comparative cost—denying a target state those items which will force it to reallocate the greatest amount of its resources to produce an item needed for a given strategy. *Ibid.*, pp. 215–16.

30. U.S., Congress, Comptroller General, *The Government's Role in East-West Trade Problems and Issues, Summary Statement of Report to the Congress by the Comptroller General of the United States*, February 4, 1976, pp. 42, 43.

31. *Ibid.*

32. Senate Hearings 1976, pp. 3–5.

33. House Hearings 1977, p. 282 (prepared statement of Fredrick W. Huszagh, Executive Director, Dean Rusk Center for Comparative Law, University of Georgia).

34. "Generally speaking the bureaucracy favors little modification of the present act. There is evidence to suggest this preference results from the great latitude that the current act vests in implementing agencies. . . .

"In summary, there is considerable lack of agreement among the various agencies as to what is currently mandated by Congress, *and there is little evidence that attempts are being made to reconcile these differences or to engage in a full exchange with Congress* to bring clarity to these issues. . . . Furthermore, *the executive branch agencies apparently find some currency in this confusion, and seem unwilling to support legislative reforms that would bring clarity to both policy objectives or procedures to be employed for their implementation.*" *Ibid.*, p. 285 (emphasis added).

35. House Hearings 1977, p. 242.

36. *Ibid.*

37. While congressional oversight would appear to be a more promising means of controlling the licensing process, its potential impact was limited by its political unattractiveness. Politically, oversight was described by one congressional insider as a "no-win" situation for Congress. The public was generally uninterested in oversight. Furthermore, the technical nature of export control licensing makes it a subject both difficult for the public to understand and easy for the public to misunderstand. Hence, the general mood of détente and the complexity of export control licensing prevented either general public interest or political benefit from oversight efforts. The system's complexity also created the possibility that congressional oversight would be interpreted by some voters as endangering the executive's efforts to protect national security.

5. Executive Autonomy and Foreign Policy Export Controls

1. *Export Administration Act of 1969*, Pub. L. 91-184, 83 Stat. 841, sec. 3(2)(B) (1969); *Export Control Act of 1949*, 63 Stat. 7 (1949).

2. Trade embargoes imposed against North Korea, Cuba, and Vietnam are examples of former "national security" controls which have become controls maintained expressly for foreign policy purposes.

The national security origins of such controls were discussed in the testimony of William A. Root, Director, Office of East-West Trade, Department of State: "The North Korean embargo was initiated to assist in the prosecution of the Korean war. It continues in order to deny military material, economic benefits, and contact that might be taken as implied recognition.

"The Vietnam embargo was imposed originally to assist in the prosecution of the war in that country. The United States is prepared to lift the embargo once relations are normalized and embassies are in place.

"Controls are maintained on exports to Kampuchea—or Cambodia as we think it—as the only practical step open to us to encourage the emergence of an independent and neutral nation responsive to the needs and rights of the people.

"In Cuba, controls imposed originally because of a severe deterioration in our political and economic relations are maintained to press the Cuban Government to show restraint in Africa." U.S., Congress, House, Committee on Foreign Affairs, *Extension and Revision of the Export Administration Act of 1969*, 96th Cong., 1st sess., 1979, p. 132 (hereafter House Hearings 1979).

3. The Rhodesian ban was lifted in 1979 by a United Nations Security Council resolution.

4. U.S., Department of Commerce, "Restrictions on Exports to the Republic of South Africa and Namibia," 43 *Federal Register* 7311, 1978.

5. These controls were introduced for human rights purposes in February 1978. See U.S., Department of Commerce, "Restriction on Exports to the Republic of South Africa and Namibia," 43 *Federal Register* 7311, February 22, 1978. The policy marked a significant extension of the arms embargo directed by the United Nations in the fall of 1977.

6. These controls were imposed by the Carter administration during a strain in U.S.-Soviet relations following the trial of Soviet dissidents. U.S., Department of Commerce, "Controls on Exports of Petroleum Equipment to the U.S.S.R., Estonia, Latvia, and Lithuania," 43 *Federal Register* 33,699, August 1, 1978. The controls introduced on this date required a validated license on U.S. exports to the Soviet Union of products and technology related to oil and gas exploration and production. The controls applied not only to exports and reexports of U.S.-origin products and technology but also to exports by foreign licensees

of products made with U.S.-origin technical data. Thus, controls introduced at this time potentially affected not only direct U.S.-Soviet trade, but, like many other U.S. controls, had a potentially significant extraterritorial impact. These controls were not exercised to the fullest extent until the pipeline embargo under the Reagan administration.

7. In October 1978, Congress, not the President, prohibited export to Uganda of products and technical data until the President determined and certified to Congress that the Ugandan government was no longer committing a consistent pattern of gross violations of human rights. *Bretton Woods Agreement Amendments Act*, Pub. L. 95-435, 92 Stat. 1051, sec. 5(a) (1978) (repealed 1979).

8. U.S., Department of Commerce, "Revision of Export Administration Regulations in Support of Human Rights," 43 *Federal Register* 27,985–86, June 28, 1978.

9. See U.S., Congress, Senate, Committee on Banking, Housing, and Urban Affairs, *Export Control Policy and Extension of the Export Administration Act*, 96th Cong., 1st sess., 1979, p. 211, n. 106 (statement of Richard Cooper).

The executive also used its authority to deny particular licenses as a form of foreign policy export control. Perhaps the most famous example was President Carter's decision in July 1978 to deny Sperry Rand Corporation's application for a license to export a Sperry Univac computer to TASS, the official Soviet news agency, for coverage of the 1980 Olympic games in Moscow. The President's decision, made at the urging of the National Security Council, protested the Soviet Union's arrest and trial of an American businessman on charges of violating Soviet currency laws and the trial and sentencing of Soviet dissidents Anatoly Scharansky and Aleksandr Ginzburg.

10. The promotion abroad of internationally recognized human rights had become a major objective of U.S. foreign policy, which, while recognized in a variety of other U.S. trade and aid statues, never became a formal goal of the Export Administration Act.

11. *Export Administration Act of 1969*, Pub. L. 91-184, 83 Stat. 841 sec. 3(1) (1969).

12. *Arms Export Control Act of 1968*, 22 U.S.C. secs. 2751–94 (1976 & Supp. III 1979).

13. The United States' COCOM allies did not join in the above-mentioned foreign policy export control programs of the Carter administration.

14. J. Kenneth Fasick, International Division, General Accounting Office, summarized the conclusion reached with regard to foreign policy export control reporting requirements in *Export Controls: Need to Clarify Policy and Simplify Administration, Report to the Congress by the Comptroller General of the United States:* "In our most recent report we noted that the Congress is not regularly and systematically informed

about how and why foreign policy controls are being used. The Congress does not have an adequate basis for evaluating the merit of such controls, much less the impact they have on international trade."

He continued by suggesting that, although the current Export Administration Act required Commerce to prepare a semiannual report to the Congress and the President on the use of controls, "the discussion on controls for foreign policy purposes in this report is brief and we believe inadequate because it does not discuss: one, the specific foreign policy goals that trade controls are supposedly designed to serve nor, two, whether they are serving these goals well or poorly." House Hearings 1979, p. 259.

15. *Export Administration Act of 1979*, Pub L. 96-72, 93 Stat. 503 (1979).

16. Congress noted that licensing delays and overly inclusive lists of controlled commodities resulted in continuing inefficiencies in licensing practices: "This legislation is also necessary to improve the efficiency of export licensing and to provide for periodic and systematic review and revision of export control policy to insure that controls are achieving their intended purposes, are not excessive, and are focused on items for which export control is most important to the national interest." House Hearings 1979, p. 2. See discussion in chapter 4.

17. U.S., Congress, Senate, S. Rept. 169, 96th Cong., 1st sess., 1979, p. 3 (hereafter Senate Report 1979).

18. *Ibid.*

19. See, for example, House Hearings 1979, p. 504 (statements of Thomas A. Christiansen of Hewlett-Packard, representing the American Electronics Association; and Robert McLellan, Vice President, FMC Corporation, and Chairman of the National Association of Manufacturers' International Trade Subcommittee).

20. Several recent policy studies on the use of economic sanctions for foreign policy purposes reached a similar conclusion, i.e., that such policies are of little effect in achieving their stated or implied policy objective, but do serve a variety of alternative purposes. For example, Daoudi and Dajani list seven alternative goals of economic sanctions:

(1) Maintaining the perception that sanctions are inflicting damage on the target;
(2) Expressing morality and justice;
(3) Signaling disapproval or displeasure;
(4) Satisfying the moral needs of sanctioners;
(5) Maintaining the sanctioner's positive image and reputation;
(6) Relieving domestic pressure on the sanctioner; and
(7) Inflicting symbolic vengeance.

M. S. Daoudi and M. S. Dajani, *Economic Sanctions: Ideals and Experience*, p. 161.

Hufbauer and Schott point out that the "demonstration of resolve" has often supplied the driving force behind the imposition of American sanctions. They continue: "United States presidents seemingly feel compelled to dramatize their opposition to foreign misdeeds, even when the likelihood of changing behavior in the target country seems remote. In these cases sanctions often are imposed because the cost of inaction—in lost confidence at home and abroad in the ability or willingness of the U.S. to act—is seen as greater than the cost of the sanctions.

"Indeed, such action is often expected by the international community—to demonstrate moral outrage and to reassure its allies that the United States will stand by its international commitments. The impact of such moral and psychological factors on the decision to impose sanctions should not be underestimated, even if it is hard to document." Gary C. Hufbauer and Jeffrey J. Schott, *Economic Sanctions in Support of Foreign Policy Goals*, p. 10.

21. See Senate Report 1979, p. 6 (Statement of former Under Secretary of State George Ball); *ibid.* (Statement of former Under Secretary of Defense David Packard).

22. U.S., Congress, House, H.R. 2539, 96th Cong., 1st sess., 1979, sec. 6(b).

23. *Ibid.* The business community, while appreciative of the intent of requirements for consultation with industry and notification to Congress, stated: "We do not believe such provisions are preferable to a simple, strong criteria formulation limiting the grant of authority for this type of control." Moreover, business leaders suggested that the 1979 act should stipulate a variety of stricter procedural requirements, including a public comment period for nonemergency controls, a report by the executive to Congress *before* controls are implemented, and an a priori congressional approval for any proposed controls. *Ibid.*, pp. 1061–62, 1091.

24. House Hearings 1979, p. 224 (statement of James A. Gray, President, National Machine Tool Builders' Association).

25. *Ibid.*, p. 255. The same recommendation was made by the National Association of Manufacturers: "We suggest that the approach used in the military security export control section be followed, where the determination of foreign availability is decisive in weighing the likely effectiveness and advisability of an export control restriction. The same approach should be applied regarding foreign policy export controls, so that failure to meet the specified criteria would preclude the use of such controls." *Ibid.*, p. 1091 (statement of Robert McLellan).

26. The Department of Defense questioned the need for imposing new or rigid export control criteria based on foreign availability tests as proposed in the new legislation and added "we consider existing

legislation as quite adequate in that regard." House Hearings 1979, p. 632.

27. For example, the State Department indicated in a letter to Senator William Proxmire, Chairman of the Committee rewriting the statute: "Factors such as these are now taken into consideration. However, legislation would be undesirable because of the need for Executive Branch flexibility in reacting to the extreme acts of other Governments contrary to our interests. . . .

"We may wish to distance ourselves from extreme acts of other Governments, such as apartheid or the suspected development of a nuclear weapons capability, even if the only short-term trade effect of our controls might be to divert export sales to our competitors." Senate Report 1979, p. 8.

Similarly, the Commerce Department asserted that it had considered foreign availability in its most recent foreign policy sanctions against the Soviet Union involving oil and gas equipment and a computer destined for the TASS news service. But it also stressed the importance of maintaining flexibility in its policy regardless of foreign availability: "We believe that the range of factors that needs to be considered is so broad that they cannot possibly be spelled out in their entirety in the statutory provision. In many circumstances, *it may be necessary to disregard certain criteria in the application of foreign policy controls because of particular circumstances.* For example, there may be circumstances in which we wish to disassociate the United States from a particular regime. *In these circumstances, the question of the enforceability of the control, and other factors become irrelevant.* We are proposing, as I indicated before, to weigh foreign availability when considering the imposition of the foreign policy controls.

"Beyond that, Mr. Chairman, *it is the administration's position that further criteria would hamstring the administration and would not give the administration necessary flexibility in certain circumstances.*" House Hearings 1979, p. 685 (emphases added).

28. "The second issue, Mr. Chairman is the proposal to provide for congressional veto of foreign policy controls. The administration opposes such a provision. . . ." *Ibid.*, p. 685 (statement of Stanley Marcuss, Senior Deputy Assistant Secretary for Industry and Trade, Department of Commerce).

"The fourth point is a proposal to require prior consultation with industry and prior negotiation with foreign governments before imposing foreign policy export controls. What we object to is the prior requirement." *Ibid.*, p. 687.

29. "The Administration . . . believes that such congressional vetoes are unconstitutional and violate the separation of powers clause. Such provisions interfere with the flexibility necessary to conduct foreign policy." *Ibid.*, p. 685.

30. Senate Report 1979, p. 3.
31. See *Export Administration Act of 1979*, Pub. L. 96-72, 93 Stat. 503, sec. 3(10) (1979).
32. *Ibid.*, sec. 4(c).
33. Senate Report 1979, p. 8.
34. *Ibid.*, p. 9.
35. *Ibid.*, p. 8.
36. *Export Administration Act of 1979.* sec. 6(b) (1979).
37. See House Hearings 1979, pt. 1, pp. 685–86 (statement of Stanley Marcuss).
38. Senate Report 1979, p. 8.
39. *Ibid.*
40. *Export Administration Act of 1979*, Pub. L. 96-72, 93 Stat. 503, secs. 6(c), (d) (1979).
41. *Ibid.*, sec. 6(e).
42. The conference report to the 1979 act states: "In agreeing to eliminate the House provision for a Congressional veto by concurrent resolution of new forms of export controls for foreign policy purposes, the conferees emphasize this expectation that the executive branch would consult fully with Congress prior to employing such controls, and agreed to give further consideration to a congressional veto mechanism in subsequent legislation in the event prior consultation on foreign policy export controls proved inadequate under the provisions of this act." H.R. Con. Rept. 482, 96th Cong., 1st sess. (1979).
43. Representative Clement Zablocki, (D-N.Y.), for example, was particularly adamant in demanding that the executive comply with the consultation and reporting requirements of the 1979 act.
44. U.S., Department of Commerce, "Revisions to Reflect Identification and Continuation of Foreign Policy Export Controls," 45 *Federal Register* 1595, January 1, 1980.
45. U.S., Department of Commerce, "Restrictions on the Export of Agricultural Commodities & Products to the U.S.S.R.," 45 *Federal Register* 1883, January 9, 1980.
46. U.S., Department of Commerce, "Commodity Control List: Restriction on the Export of Marketable Phosphate Rock, Phosphate Acid of All Concentration, and Processed Phosphatic Fertilizers of All Concentrations to the U.S.S.R.," 45 *Federal Register* 8293, February 7, 1980. See also "East-West Trade: Carter Indefinitely Suspends Phosphate Exports to the Soviet Union," *U.S. Export Weekly*, 296 (February 26, 1980) A16.
47. See Memorandum for the Secretary of Commerce Prohibiting Transactions with Respect to the Summer Olympic Games in Moscow (March 28, 1980), reprinted in *U.S. Export Weekly* (April 1, 1980) p. N-1.
48. U.S., Department of Commerce, "Revision of Policy on Exports to Afghanistan," 45 *Federal Register* 37,415, June 3, 1980.

49. U.S., Department of Commerce, "Restrictions on Exports for the Kama River Truck Complex in the U.S.S.R. of Truck Engine Assembly Lines," 45 *Federal Register* 30,617, May 9, 1980.

50. In December 1977, Congress passed the International Emergency Economic Powers Act (IEEPA). The grant of authority to the President under IEEPA was similar substantively to that given to the President under section 5(b) of the Trading with the Enemy Act. It provides that in case of any "unusual and extraordinary threat, which has its source in whole or in substantial part outside the United States, to the national security, foreign policy, or economy of the United States," the President may declare a national emergency with respect to such a threat and may:

(A) investigate, regulate, or prohibit
  (i) any transaction in foreign exchange;
  (ii) any transfers of credit or payments between, by or to any banking institution, to the extent that such transfers or payments involve any interest of any foreign country or national thereof;
  (iii) the importing or exporting of currency or securities; and
(B) investigate, regulate, direct and compel, nullify, void, prevent or prohibit, any acquisition, holding, withholding, use, transfer, withdrawal, transportation, importation or exportation of, or dealings in, or exercising any right, power, or privilege with respect to, or transaction involving any property in which any foreign country or a national thereof, has any interest; by any person, or with respect to any property, subject to the jurisdiction of the United States.

50 U.S.C. sec. 1702.

Procedurally, however, the International Emergency Powers Act imposed a variety of new requirements on the executive. Under the IEEPA, the President must declare a national emergency in conformity with the provisions of the National Emergency Act, and the emergency must constitute an "unusual and extraordinary threat. . . ." The President is required to consult, if possible, with Congress before invoking the act and must, upon exercising his powers under the IEEPA, send a report to Congress to be supplemented every six months for the duration of the emergency.

51. See *Congressional Quarter Weekly Report*, January 26, 1980, p. 199.

52. These were largely bipartisan concerns. For example, Senator Howard Baker (R-Tenn.) noted that suspending U.S. grain exports "is not a very useful tool of foreign policy." A U.S. agricultural embargo would, in Baker's estimation, "starve the wrong people, hurt U.S. traders and farmers" and is "offensive to the moral character of the U.S. people." Senator Adlai Stevenson (D-Ill.) stated that export em-

bargoes "produce exports of U.S. jobs and capital" and that economic warfare would be unlikely to influence Soviet politics. "East-West Trade: Carter Announces Trade Response to Soviet Invasion of Afghanistan," *U.S. Export Weekly* (January 8, 1980) 289:A6; "Export Controls: Administration Testimony Alluding to Shift in Policy Raises Concern in Congress," *U.S. Export Weekly* (January 9, 1980) 292:A3.

53. A variety of events in the United States and abroad threatened to undermine the effectiveness and the remaining public support for the controls. In 1980, the U.S. Department of Agriculture's (USDA's) statistics confirmed what many critics of the embargo had maintained; that the Soviet Union was obtaining significantly more grain than the administration had initially forecast and that the potential effect of the embargo on the U.S. farm sector was significant. A record 1979 grain harvest and increases in farm machinery and input costs led the USDA to forecast a 20 percent decline in 1980 farm income—before the embargo had been declared. The embargo, it estimated, would reduce farm income by an additional $3 billion with no offsetting benefits to U.S. consumers.

In addition, the administration's decisions to honor its commitment to sell 8 million metric tons of grain to the Soviet Union in 1980 and to permit U.S. grain-trading companies to sell non-U.S. grain through their foreign subsidies eroded much of the remaining support for the embargo. See U.S., Congress, House, Committee on Foreign Affairs, *An Assessment of the Afghanistan Sanctions: Implications for Trade and Diplomacy in the 1980s,* 97th Cong., 1st sess. (1981), pp. 23–52.

54. While Agriculture Secretary John Block urged the President to rescind the embargo immediately, Secretary of State Haig, among others, believed that lifting the embargo while Soviet troops remained in Afghanistan and were poised on the Polish border would send the wrong signal to the USSR. *Ibid.*

55. See U.S., General Accounting Office, *Administration Knowledge of Economic Costs of Foreign Policy Controls,* September 2, 1983, p. 3.

56. See "House Bill Would End Foreign Policy Curbs on Oil and Gas Equipment to the Soviet Union," *U.S. Export Weekly* (June 15, 1982), 412:404. The bill was later revised to cover both phases of the pipeline controls. Representative Findley stated, "Simply these sanctions have never worked and they will not work in the future. The Soviet pipeline will be built, and American companies will continue to suffer because of unilateral sanctions that do not have the support of our allies." "Legislation Introduced in House Would Repeal Soviet Foreign Policy Controls," *U.S. Export Weekly* (July 27, 1982), 417:609.

57. PBS, "MacNeil/Lehrer Report," June 21, 1982.

58. *Facts on File World News Digest,* June 25, 1982, p. 459.

59. The Export Administration Act has always contained authority for some extraterritorial extension of U.S. law. Before 1977, the regu-

lations published pursuant to the Export Administration Act controlled the reexport of U.S.-origin goods or technology by a foreign company, export of foreign-origin goods that include U.S.-origin parts or components, and exports of foreign-origin goods that are products of U.S.-origin technology.

In 1977, Congress transferred nonemergency, nonwartime extraterritorial export control authority from section 5(b) of the Trading with the Enemy Act, by amendment to the Export Administration Act. The amendment expanded the jurisdictional reach of the Export Administration Act to include authority to control the disposition of goods by any person subject to the jurisdiction of the United States. See U.S., Congress, House, H. Rept. 459, 95th Cong., 1st sess., 1977, p. 21.

The permissive language remained intact during passage of the 1979 Export Administration Act, even though Congress had begun to recognize that the possible exercise of this broad jurisdictional authority could infringe another state's sovereignty under international law and create political problems for the United States. See for example, U.S., Congress, Committee on Foreign Affairs, *Extension and Revision of the Export Administration Act of 1969*, 96th Cong. 1st sess., 1979, p. 1059 (letter of Charles W. Stewart, President, Machinery and Allied Products Institute, to Jonathan B. Bingham, Chairman, Subcommittee on International Economic Policy and Trade, House Committee on Foreign Affairs). The Senate Committee on Banking, Housing, and Urban Affairs considered but rejected limiting the jursidictional reach of the act in deference to the executive's claims that it needed such powers to effectively and flexibly implement foreign policy export controls. U.S., Congress, Senate, S. Rept. 169 to Accompany S. 737, 96th Cong., 1st sess., 1979, p. 5.

60. Letter in private collection, Washington, D.C.

61. The executive's awareness of the Europeans' opposition to the pipeline controls is discussed in detail in Alexander M. Haig., Jr., *Caveat*, pp. 239–56. The initial phase of the controls contained the traditional extraterritorial aspects of control over the reexport of licensed goods and technology.

62. First, the extended pipeline controls made the earlier restrictions applicable to all exports to the Soviet Union by foreign firms owned or controlled by U.S. individuals or corporations, even if no U.S.-origin technology or components were involved. Second, products and technology exported by wholly foreign-owned or foreign-controlled companies were also controlled if the pipeline equipment was manufactured under a license, contract, or royalty arrangement with a U.S. company that required the foreign manufacturer to comply with U.S. export regulations. This control applied to U.S. components or technology received by the foreign corporation *before* the initiation of pipeline controls. In the past, controls over exports of foreign products

based upon U.S. technology had been asserted only prospectively. Foreign goods were subject to U.S. export control laws only when the acquisition of the underlying technology was subject to controls and the foreign importer had assured the exporter, in writing, that he did not intend to reexport products of the controlled technology to a proscribed destination.

The pipeline regulations represented the first retroactive foreign policy export controls; foreign licensees of U.S.-origin technology were prohibited from exporting the products of that technology, even though the technology was not restricted when it was originally acquired. The practical effect of such controls was not merely to stop exports from the United States to the Soviet Union but to stop the French firm of Alsthom-Atlantique—the only non-U.S. firm with turbine rotor manufacturing capability critical to the completion of the pipeline—from exporting to the Soviet Union even though the French concern had licensed its technology from General Electric long before the President issued the pipeline controls.

63. For reaction in the press, see, for example, "Common Market Challenges U.S. Policies on Trade as Economic Relations Worsen," *Wall Street Journal*, August 10, 1982, p. 42.

Formal comments included the following: "The European Community wishes to draw attention to the importance that it attaches to the legal, political and economic aspects of the United States' measure, including their impact on the commercial policy of the Community. As to the legal aspects, the European Community considers the U.S. measures contrary to international law, and apparently at variance with rules and principles laid down in U.S. law.

"As to the political and economic aspects, it is clear that the U.S. measures are liable to affect a wide variety of business activities while their primary purpose is to delay the construction of the pipeline to bring Soviet gas to Western Europe. . . . Whatever the effect on the Soviet Union, the effects on European Community interest of the U.S. measure, applied retroactively and without sufficient consultation, are unquestionably and seriously damaging." *Comments of the European Community on the Amendments of June 22, 1982 to the U.S. Export Administration Regulations*, August 12, 1982 (mimeo).

See also "France Defies the U.S. Ban on Gear for Soviet's Gas Pipeline to Europe," *Wall Street Journal*, July 23, 1982, p. 20; "Italy Follows French Stance on Pipeline," *Wall Street Journal*, July 26, 1982, p. 2; "Britain Orders 4 Firms to Defy U.S. Pipeline Ban," *Wall Street Journal*, August 3, 1982, p. 37.

The British Government, acting pursuant to its own legislation, the Protection of Trading Interests Act, threatened a British company and three British subsidiaries of U.S. companies with penalties under the act should they fail to honor their contracts because of the extraterritorial extension of the U.S. export control regulations. France ordered its companies to comply with the terms of their contract. See Great Britain, *Protection of Trading Interests Order, 1982.* Complaint for Declaratory and Injunctive Relief, *Dresser Industries, Inc. v. Baldrige,* 549 F. Supp. 108 (D.D.C. 1982) (Exhibit 2).

64. See U.S., Congress, Library of Congress, Congressional Research Service, *Soviet Pipeline, Report Prepared by Congressional Research Service of the Library of Congress,* p. 3.

65. For an overview of Western European reactions to the Polish crisis and views on East-West relations see generally, Herbert J. Ellison, ed., *Soviet Policy Toward Western Europe.*

66. The first direct challenge to U.S. authority came at the end of August when the French government ordered Dresser (France), a wholly owned subsidiary of Dresser Industries (an American corporation), to fulfill its pipeline contract. When Dresser (France) exported compressors to the Soviet Union in violation of U.S. export controls, the U.S. Department of Commerce, pursuant to its administrative enforcement authority under the Export Administration Act and regulations, placed the company on the "temporary denial list." This denial list prohibited Dresser Industries and its subsidiaries from participating, directly or indirectly, in any export transaction involving U.S.-origin oil and gas goods or technology and revoked its outstanding validated export licenses. Dresser Industries challenged the validity of the regulations through an administrative appeal within the Commerce Department and by bringing suit in federal district court. Pending resolution of the Dresser Industries suit, several other French, British, German, and Italian firms shipped pipeline goods and technology to the Soviet Union in contravention of the American regulations, leading to their placement on the denial list as well.

Although dropped when President Reagan lifted the sanctions, in their administrative and judicial protests, the European firms challenged the regulations as actions beyond the authority delegated to the President under the Export Administration Act, contrary to international law, and in violation of the due process clause of the Constitution. The merits of these claims will not be discussed in detail here. Some jurists who have considered the legality of U.S. pipeline controls have concluded that the President's actions were not justified under existing basis of jurisdiction under international law. See, for example, Compagnie Européene des Petroles S. A. v. Sensor Nederland B.V., wherein the District Court of the Hague found that none of the established jurisdictional principles of international law justified the second phase of the pipeline regulations. *International Legal Materials* (1983) 22:66.

67. See, for example, a statement by the Caterpillar Tractor Company on the effects of the pipeline controls, in which Caterpillar claimed an immediate loss of a sale of 200 pipelayers with a license value of

$90 million. U.S., Congress, Joint Economic Committee, *Soviet Pipeline Sanctions: the European Perspective*, 97th Cong., 2d sess., 1982, pp. 5–7. Caterpillar further claimed that cancellation of this contract cost them additional related sales, undermined its international price competitiveness by the loss of the Soviet market, and damaged its reputation and the reputation of other U.S. companies as reliable suppliers. *Ibid.*

Senator Roger Jepsen (R-Iowa) noted that opposition of the American business community to the pipeline controls was widespread and that the executive was aware of business's attitude: "In response to the Commerce Department request for comments under the provisions of the Export Administration Act, the executive branch has received reams and reams of material from firms cataloging the injuries. A Pennsylvania firm writes it could lose an order for $800,000 in spare parts under technology originally transferred to Europe in the early 1960's. Another $2 million in new business—none of it for use in the pipeline—could be lost to other suppliers.

"A large multinational has lost contracts worth $75 million, accounting for 1,000 man-years of employment in parent company U.S. factories and another 1,000 in factories of U.S.-based contractors. Dresser Industries has laid off 7,500 people in the United States and Canada and, since early 1982, has turned away $100 million in orders unrelated to the pipeline. Another Texas firm has clients with approximately $33 million in customized manufactured equipment under contract; that equipment may now be undeliverable." *Ibid.*, p. 3.

Mr. Andre Fontaine, Editor of *Le Monde*, summarized the European position at this time: "it is not France only who is in opposition to U.S. policy, but that the main European countries—West Germany, Britain, France, and Italy—stand on the same line on the pipeline issue." U.S. Congress, Joint Economic Committee, *Soviet Pipeline Sanctions: The European Perspective*, 97th Cong., 2d sess., 1982, p. 10.

68. A Gallup poll taken in August 1982 posed the following questions to a representative sample of the American public: "Have you heard or read about the Reagan Administration's attempt to prevent our allies from supplying U.S. equipment and technology to build a natural gas pipeline between the Soviet Union and Western Europe? (Asked of those who had heard or read about the Reagan policy): Would you say you approve or disapprove of the Administration's position on this matter?"

The result of the poll revealed that 52 percent of those questioned had heard or read about the policy and of that number 48 percent approved of it, 42 percent opposed it, and 10 percent expressed no opinion. "U.S. Policy Toward European Gas Pipeline," *Gallup Report* (August 1982), 203:13.

A House of Representatives bill was introduced by Representative

Paul Findley (R-Ill.) on July 22, 1982, to repeal the pipeline controls. A similar bill was introduced in the Senate by Senator Paul Tsongas (D-Mass.) on August 13, 1982. The House bill was narrowly defeated (206 to 203) and the Senate bill did not reach a vote because the President lifted the sanctions before the Senate could reconvene to consider the legislation. See Homer E. Moyer and Linda A. Mabry, "Export Controls as Instruments of Foreign Policy: The History, Legal Issues, and Policy Lessons of Three Recent Cases," p. 73.

69. Controls on oil exploration and transmission were not completely lifted in 1982. In 1987, the executive lifted foreign policy controls over oil exploration and production equipment; and despite their classification as transmission equipment, pipelayers remained on the Commodity Control List with exploration and production equipment until August 1983.

70. The United States, under President Carter, imposed foreign policy controls on exports to Libya of off-highway wheel tractors, crime control equipment, large aircraft and helicopters, and certain other commodities and technical data. 43 *Federal Register* 20,484, 1978.

71. See generally 15 C.F.R. secs. 379.4, 385.7 (1984).

72. Two additions to the foreign policy controls governing exports to Iran and Iraq were made during 1984 and later modified.

73. Philip Klutznick, Secretary of Commerce, to Congress, Extending and Expanding Foreign Policy Controls, December 31, 1980.

74. As reflected in the text of the report, the Commerce Department offered no substantive discussion of the significance or effectiveness of foreign policy controls:

(1) Although in many cases, foreign availability of comparable goods will limit the impact of [antiterrorism] controls, the controls demonstrate the firm determination of the United States to oppose and distance itself from acts of international terrorism.

   Judicious application of export controls in conjunction with other efforts has served to enhance our overall effort to combat international terrorism.

(2) Although the effectiveness of the [crime control and detection] controls in denying exports is limited by the availability of comparable goods from other countries, governments which want to preserve a security relationship with the U.S. have shown a willingness to make sure, at least marginal adjustments in respect to human rights. Moreover, these controls help distance the U.S. government from some repressive regimes.

(3) Despite foreign availability, the [South African] controls constitute a significant unilateral declaration of U.S. unwillingness to aid and abet the South African Government policy of institutionalized racial discrimination.

(4) Controls on the export to Libya of off-highway wheel tractors with a carriage capacity of ten tons or more are designed to further the foreign policy objective of regional stability. Tractors under these controls can be used to transport tanks and other outsized military vehicles and would thereby enhance the mobility of Libya's sizable armored forces. Foreign availability is a major deterrent to the effectiveness of these controls.

(5) In each case, although the availability of foreign goods limits the extent to which the [North Korean, Vietnamese, Kampuchean, and Cuban] controls deny exports to these countries, the embargoes should not be lifted except as part of a general improvement of relations.

U.S., Department of Commerce, Office of Export Administration, *Foreign Policy Report to Congress*, December 31, 1980.

75. "Banking Committee Members Hit Foreign Policy Controls Report," *U.S. Export Weekly* (March 30, 1982), 401:763.

76. *Ibid.*, p. 765.

77. Compare with note 74 above the following:

(1) Although in many cases foreign availability of comparable goods will limit the impact of these [antiterrorism] controls, the controls demonstrate the firm determination of the United States to oppose and distance itself from acts of international terrorism.

Judicious application of export controls in conjunction with other efforts has served to enhance our overall effort to combat international terrorism.

(2) The effectiveness of the controls on crime control and detection equipment is limited by the availability of comparable goods from foreign sources. The symbolic aspect of the controls is an important element of their effectiveness. Denying exports of such goods to countries that continually violate internationally recognized human rights helps distance the U.S. government from countries about which we have human rights concerns.

(3) Given foreign availability of U.S.-controlled products and technical data ... these [South African] controls will not in many cases prevent South African access to similar goods from other sources. The controls do represent constant and firm evidence of continued U.S. unwillingness to aid and abet the South African policy of institutionalized racial discrimination.

(4) Foreign availability is a major deterrent to the effectiveness of these controls [on the export to Libya of off-highway wheel tractors]. The controls nonetheless restrict an American contribution to Libyan military activities.

(5) In each case, although the availability of foreign goods limits

the extent to which the [North Korean, Vietnamese, Kampuchean, and Cuban] controls deny exports to these countries, the embargoes should not be lifted except as part of a general improvement of relations.

U.S., Department of Commerce, Office of Export Administration, *Foreign Policy Report to Congress*, January 18, 1985.

78. See U.S., General Accounting Office, *Administration Knowledge of Economic Costs of Foreign Policy Export Controls*, September 2, 1983, pp. 16–23.

79. See U.S., Department of Commerce, *Export Administration Annual Report for the Fiscal Year 1980*, p. 8.

80. See U.S. General Accounting Office, *Administration Knowledge of Economic Costs*, pp. 16–23.

81. *Ibid.*

82. *Ibid.*

83. U.S., Congress, Senate, *The Export Administration Act Amendments of 1983*, S. Rept. to Accompany S. 979, 98th Cong., 1st sess., 1983, p. 14.

84. *Ibid.*, p. 13.

85. *Ibid.* As a result, the Export Administration Amendments Act of 1985 amended this section to provide that the President may impose, expand, or extend foreign policy export controls only if he makes specific *determinations*, rather than merely *considers* the criteria listed in section 6(b), and sets a six-month expiration date for all foreign policy export controls unilaterally imposed by the United States. *Export Administration Amendments Act of 1985*, Pub. L. 99-64, 99 Stat. 120 (1985), sec. 108(b).

86. Specifically, section 6(e) of the 1979 act provides: "Notification to Congress—The President in every possible instance shall consult with the Congress *before* imposing any export control under this section . . . whenever the President imposes, expands, or extends export controls under this section, the President *shall immediately notify* the Congress of such action and shall submit with such notification a report specifying—

(1) The conclusions of the President with respect to each of the criteria set forth in subsection (b); and
(2) The nature and results of any alternative means attempted under subsection (d), or the reasons for imposing, extending or expanding the control without attempting any such alternative means.

"Such report shall also indicate how such controls will further significantly the foreign policy of the United States or will further its declared international obligations" (emphasis added).

87. Malcolm Baldrige, Secretary of Commerce, to the Honorable

George Bush, President of the Senate, June 23, 1982, reprinted in *Export Administration Annual Report for the Fiscal Year 1982*, p. 162.

88. *Ibid.*, p. 169.

89. U.S., Congress, Senate, *The Export Administration Act Amendments of 1983*, S. Rept. to Accompany S. 979, 98th Cong., 1st sess., 1983, p. 14.

90. U.S., Congress, Senate, Committee on Banking, Housing, and Urban Affairs, *Reauthorization of the Export Administration Act*, 98th Cong., 1st sess., 1983, pp. 745, 759.

91. *Export Administration Amendments Act of 1985*, sec. 108.

6. Recent Developments in Export Control Policy

1. The January 1985 directive authorized the Defense Department to review export licenses concerning 7 sensitive commodity control list categories to 17 non-COCOM Western nations.

2. See for example, U.S., Congress, House, Committee on Banking, Housing, and Urban Affairs, *Reauthorization of the Export Administration Act*, 98th Cong., 1st sess., 1983 (hereafter House Hearings 1983), pp. 486–90 (testimony of Erskine C. Chapman, Executive Vice President, Caterpillar Tractor Company).

3. *Export Administration Amendments Act of 1985*, Pub. L. 99-64, 99 Stat. 120 (1985).

An unresolved deadlock between the Senate and the House in the second session of the 98th Congress had resulted in the lapse of the Export Administration Act of 1979 on March 30, 1984. The 1979 act's provisions were prolonged by the President's issuance of Executive Order 12,470 under the authority of the International Emergency Economic Powers Act.

4. U.S., Congress, General Accounting Office, *Export Controls: Assessment of Commerce Department's Foreign Policy Report to Congress* (August 1986).

5. *Ibid.*, p. 5.

6. *Ibid.*

7. *Ibid.* Similarly, the report concluded that the enforcement section "incompletely assesses" foreign policy export enforcement problems. It recommended that future reports contain more discussion of foreign policy control enforcement difficulties specifically addressed to enforcement difficulties involving reexport from third countries. *Ibid.*, p. 8.

8. See, for example, House Hearings 1983, p. 177 (statement of William Schneider, Jr., Under Secretary for Security Assistance, Science, and Technology, Department of State). The draft conference report

stated: "Extraterritorial application of U.S. export controls affecting noncontractual transactions and relationships remains a serious matter of contention with other countries, particularly with European governments, and possible ways of further limiting such effects merit continued study and consideration." U.S., Congress, House, 98th Cong., 2d sess., October 11, 1984, *Congressional Record*, vol. 130 p. H12153.

9. Paul Freedenburg, Assistant Secretary for Trade Administration at the Department of Commerce, testified to the lack of interagency coordination on foreign availability assessment. See U.S., Congress, House, Subcommittee on International Economic Policy and Trade, *Oversight of the Foreign Availability Provisions of the Export Administration Act*, 99th Cong., 2d sess., 1986.

10. 51 *Federal Register* 25,360, July 14, 1986.

11. For reasons not yet publicly explained, a Commerce Department instructional cable to the U.S. delegation at COCOM regarding decontrol of the wafering saws was recalled at the insistence of the Defense Department. The cable was redrafted by Defense, or with Defense Department guidance, and sent to COCOM the week of September 8, 1986, two months after formal certification. Interview data.

12. U.S., Congress, House, Subcommittee on International Economic Policy and Trade, *Oversight of the Foreign Availability Provisions of the Export Administration Act*, 99th Cong., 2d sess., 1986.

13. See *Washington Tariff & Trade Letter* (March 17, 1986), 6:1.

14. The GAO's July 1987 assessment of foreign policy export controls concluded that such controls were largely symbolic gestures and were imposed despite widespread foreign availability. U.S., Congress, General Accounting Office, *Export Controls: Assessment of Commerce Department's Foreign Policy Report to Congress* (Washington: GAO, July 23, 1987), pp. 4–5.

15. None of the nations participating in the economic summit supported the U.S. sanctions. West German Foreign Minister Hans-Dietrich Genscher told a news conference that his own government's position always had been that trade and economic sanctions serve no useful purpose. *International Trade Reporter*, May 8, 1985, 2:638.

On the Central American opposition, see "Mexico Joins Critics of U.S. Embargo Against Nicaragua," *Washington Post*, May 5, 1985, p. A21.

As for business interests, the chairman of the U.S. Chamber of Commerce, Frank Morsani, criticized the continued use of trade sanctions as a weapon of U.S. foreign policy. See *International Trade Reporter*, May 8, 1985 2:638. Michael Hall, Executive Vice President of the National Corn Growers Association, and John Baize, Washington Director of the American Soybean Association, spoke out strongly against the embargo. See *ibid.*, p. 639.

House Republican Leader Robert Michel (R-Ill.) criticized the embargo, noting it would reopen the argument as to the reliability of the United States as a supplier on the world market. Senator Alan Cranston (D-Calif.) and Representative Don Bonker were critical of the likely effectiveness of the embargo and concerned about its immediate and future costs. *Ibid.,* p. 638.

Representative Michael D. Barnes (D-Md.), Chairman of the House Foreign Affairs Subcommittee on Western Hemisphere Affairs, said he would summon administration witnesses to a hearing on the sanctions and called it "ludicrous" to say that the Nicaraguan situation warranted the declaration of a national emergency. See "President Orders Halt to Trade With Nicaragua," *Washington Post,* May 2, 1985, pp. A1, A35.

16. In his opening statement before a joint hearing of the International Economic Policy and Trade Subcommittee and the Western Hemisphere Affairs Subcommittee, Representative Don Bonker said there was "no evidence" the Reagan administration had complied with the congressional consultation requirements of the IEEPA. Assistant Secretary of State for Inter-American Affairs Langhorne A. Motley told the panels the administration regretted the "unfortunate oversight" in not consulting with the Bonker Subcommittee on the sanctions. When Representative Bonker asked if the State Department had consulted with the House Speaker and leadership or the chairman of ranking minority member of the Foreign Affairs Committee, Motley replied that he had consulted with the Speaker's staff and the staff of the Foreign Affairs Committee. Foreign Affairs Committee Chairman, Dante B. Fascell (D-Fla.), however, was unaware of any such consultation. *International Trade Reporter,* May 8, 1985, 2:640.

17. See *Inside U.S. Trade* (March 21, 1986), 4(12):6–7.

18. On September 9, 1985, President Reagan signed Executive Order 12532 imposing limited sanctions against South Africa. The executive order provides for the following:
   (1) Banning new loans except those for education, housing or health facilities open to all races;
   (2) Banning the export of computers, computer software, and computer technology to apartheid-implementing offices of the South African government;
   (3) Banning nuclear-related exports defined as goods and technology that would be used in nuclear production or utilization facilities (export of such goods would be allowed if they are needed for health and safety or international safeguard programs);
   (4) Implementing United Nations Security Council Resolution 558 banning import of arms, ammunition, or military vehicles produced in South Africa;
   (5) Ordering an end to trade assistance to U.S. companies doing

business in South Africa, if they do not apply the Sullivan Principles;

(6) Directing all U.S. agencies with activities in South Africa to assist black-owned businesses;

(7) Ordering U.S. officials to consult with other parties to the General Agreement on Tariffs and Trade on a U.S. prohibition of Krugerrand sales;

(8) Ordering a study of the feasibility of minting U.S. gold coins;

(9) Establishing an "advisory committee" to recommend ways to encourage peaceful change in South Africa; and

(10) Providing for increased funds for scholarships to black South Africans and for grants to human rights organizations in South Africa, including legal assistance for political prisoners.

On October 1, 1985, President Reagan signed a second executive order on South Africa (Executive Order 12535) prohibiting the import of Krugerrands into the United States.

19. *The Comprehensive Anti-Apartheid Act of 1986*, Pub. L. 99-440, 100 Stat. 1086 (1986).

20. The bill barred the import of South African iron, steel, textiles, agricultural goods, and other products, and orders the suspension of direct air travel between the United States and South Africa.

7. Patterns of Executive Authority

1. In an analysis of congressional shortcomings in foreign policy-making the Special Committee on International Relations pointed to the following factors: "deference to the Executive Branch, general disinterest in foreign policy issues, parochial considerations due to constituent and interest group pressures, and fear of 'meddling' with the national security apparatus or of taking responsibility for actions in the area. . . ." U.S. Congress, House, *Congress and Foreign Policy*, 94th Cong., 2d sess., January 2, 1977, p. 19.

2. Benjamin J. Cohen, ed., *American Foreign Economic Policy*, p. 20.

3. James N. Rosenau, *The Scientific Study of Foreign Policy*, pp. 154–69.

4. Graham T. Allison, *Essence of Decision*, pp. 78–96.

5. *Ibid.* See also Morton H. Halperin, *Bureaucratic Politics and Foreign Policy*, pp. 26–62.

6. Graham T. Allison, "Conceptual Models and the Cuban Missile Crisis," in Morton T. Halperin and Arnold Kanter, eds., *Readings in American Foreign Policy*, p. 58.

7. For an actual application of this approach to U.S. import policy see Robert E. Baldwin, *The Political Economy of U.S. Import Policy*.

BIBLIOGRAPHY

Abbott, Kenneth W. "Linking Trade to Political Goals: Foreign Policy Export Controls in the 1970s and 1980s." *Minnesota Law Review* (June 1981), vol. 65.
Act of June 30, 1942. Ch. 636, sec. 6, 56 Stat. 463 (1943).
Act of August 15, 1974. Pub. L. 93-373. 88 Stat. 445 (1974).
An Act to Expedite the Strengthening of the National Defense. Ch. 703, 54 Stat. 712, 50 U.S.C.A. 701 (1940).
Adler-Karlsson, Gunnar. *Western Economic Warfare, 1947–1967.* Stockholm: Almquist and Wiksell, 1968.
Allison, Graham T. *Essence of Decision.* Boston: Little, Brown, 1971.
Allison, Graham T. "Overview of Findings and Recommendations from Defense and Arms Control Cases." In appendices of *Commission on the Organization of the Government for the Conduct of Foreign Policy* (June 1975), vol. 4. Washington, D.C.: GPO, 1975.
Allison, Graham and Peter Szanton. *Remaking Foreign Policy: The Organizational Connection.* New York: Basic Books, 1976.
Arms Export Control Act of 1968. 22 U.S.C. secs. 2751–94. (1976 & Supp. III 1979).
Ayubi, Shaheen. *Economic Sanctions in U.S. Foreign Policy.* Philadelphia: Foreign Policy Research Institute, 1982.
Balancing the National Interest. Washington, D.C.: National Academy Press, 1987.
Baldwin, David A. *Economic Development and American Foreign Policy, 1943–1962.* Chicago: University of Chicago Press, 1966.
Baldwin, David A. *Economic Statecraft.* Princeton: Princeton University Press, 1985.
Baldwin, Robert E. *The Political Economy of U.S. Import Policy.* Cambridge, Mass.: MIT Press, 1985.
"Banking Committee Members Hit Foreign Policy Controls Report." *U.S. Export Weekly* (March 30, 1982), 401:763–65.

Bauer, Raymond, Ithiel de Sola Pool, and Lewis Dexter. *American Business and Public Policy.* Chicago: Aldine-Atherton, 1972.

Berman, Harold J. "The Export Administration Act of 1969: Analysis and Appraisal." *American Review of East-West Trade* (1970), vol. 3.

Berman, Harold J. and John R. Garson. "United States Export Controls—Past, Present, and Future." *Columbia Law Review* (May 1977), vol. 67.

Bertsch, Gary K. "Western Strategic Trade Controls: Goals, Policies, Politics, and the Future." Paper prepared for the Conference on East-West Economic Relations in a Changing World Economy. Toronto, June 13–15, 1984.

Blackstone, Robert A. "U.S. Export Controls." Paper presented at Symposium of the Georgetown University Law Center for Continuing Legal Education. Washington, D.C., 1984.

Block, F. "Cooperation and Conflicts in the Capitalist World Economy." *Marxist Perspective* (1979), vol. 2.

Bretton Woods Agreement Amendments Act. Pub. L. 94-435. 92 Stat. 1051 (1978) (repealed 1979).

"Britain Orders Four Firms to Defy U.S. Pipeline Ban." *Wall Street Journal,* August 3, 1982, p. 37.

Carnoy, Martin. *The State and Political Theory.* Princeton: Princeton University Press, 1984.

Carroll, Holbert N. *The House of Representatives and Foreign Affairs.* Pittsburgh: University of Pittsburgh Press, 1958.

Cohen, Benjamin J., ed. *American Foreign Economic Policy.* New York: Harper and Row, 1968.

"Comment, the Trading with the Enemy Act of 1917 and Foreign Based Subsidiaries of American Multinational Corporations: A Time to Abstain from Restraining." *San Diego Law Review* (1973), vol. 11.

Comments of the European Community on the Amendments of June 22, 1982 to the U.S. Export Administration Regulations. August 12, 1982. (Mimeo.)

"Common Market Challenges U.S. Policies on Trade as Economic Relations Worsen." *Wall Street Journal,* August 10, 1982, p. 42.

Complaint for Declaratory and Injunctive Relief. *Dresser Industries v. Baldrige,* 549 F. Supp. 108 (D.D.C. 1982) (Exhibit 2).

Comprehensive Anti-Apartheid Act of 1986, Pub. L. 99-440. 100 Stat. 1086 (1986).

Daedalus Enterprises, Inc. v. Kreps. No. 78-893 (D.D.C. 1978).

Dahl, Robert A. *Congress and Foreign Policy.* New York: Norton, 1950.

Dahl, Robert. *Who Governs.* New Haven: Yale University Press, 1961.

Dahl, Robert A., and Charles E. Lindblom. *Politics, Economics, and Welfare.* New York: Harper, 1953.

Dam, Kenneth W. *The GATT: Law and International Economic Organization.* Chicago: University of Chicago Press, 1970.

Daoudi, M. S., and M. S. Dajani. *Economic Sanctions: Ideals and Experience.* London: Routledge and Kegan Paul, 1983.
Destler, I. M. *Making Foreign Economic Policy.* Washington, D.C.: Brookings Institution, 1980.
"*East-West Trade:* Carter Announces Trade Response to Soviet Invasion of Afghanistan." *U.S. Export Weekly* (January 8, 1980), 289:A1–A6.
"*East-West Trade:* Carter Indefinitely Suspends Phosphate Exports to the Soviet Union." *U.S. Export Weekly* (February 26, 1980), 296:A16–A17.
Ellicott, John L. "Trends in Export Regulation." *Business Lawyer* (1983), vol. 38.
Ellison, Herbert J., ed. *Soviet Policy Toward Western Europe.* Seattle: University of Washington Press, 1983.
Equal Export Opportunity Act. Pub. L. 92-412. 86 Stat. 644 (1972).
Export Administration Act of 1969. Pub. L. 91-184. 83 Stat. 841 (1969).
Export Administration Act of 1969 as amended by Equal Export Opportunity Act of 1972. Pub. L. 92-412. 86 Stat. 644 (1972).
Export Administration Act of 1974. Pub L. 93-500. 88 Stat. 1552 (1974).
Export Administration Act of 1979. Pub. L. 96-72. 93 Stat. 503 (1979).
Export Administration Amendments of 1977. Pub. L. 95-52. 91 Stat. 235 (1977).
Export Administration Amendments Act of 1985. Pub. L. 99-64. 99 Stat. 120 (1985).
Export Administration Regulations. 15 *Code of Federal Regulations*, pt. 370–99, 1987.
Export Control Act of 1949. Pub. L. 81-11. 63 Stat. 7 (1949).
"Export Controls: Administration Testimony Alluding to Shift in Policy Raises Concern in Congress." *U.S. Export Weekly* (January 29, 1980), 292: A2–A4.
"France Defies the U.S. Ban on Gear for Soviet's Gas Pipeline to Europe." *Wall Street Journal,* July 23, 1982, p. 20.
Gaddis, John Lewis. *The United States and the Origins of the Cold War, 1941–1947.* New York: Columbia University Press, 1972.
Garthoff, Raymond L. *Détente and Confrontation: American-Soviet Relations from Nixon to Reagan.* Washington, D.C.: Brookings Institution, 1985.
Goldstein, Judith L. "A Domestic Explanation for Regime Formation and Maintenance: Liberal Trade Policy in the U.S." Paper presented at the American Political Science Association, Washington, D.C., September 1984.
Goldstein, Judith L. "The Political Economy of Trade: Institutions of Protection." *American Political Science Review* (March 1986), 80:161–84.
Haig, Alexander M., Jr. *Caveat.* New York: Macmillan, 1984.

Halperin, Morton T. *Bureaucratic Politics and Foreign Policy.* Washington, D.C.: Brookings Institution, 1974.

Halperin, Morton T. and Arnold Kanter, eds., *Readings in American Foreign Policy.* Boston: Little, Brown, 1973.

Hanter, F. *Community Power Structure.* Chapel Hill: University of North Carolina Press, 1953.

Henkin, Louis. *Foreign Affairs and the Constitution.* New York: Norton, 1975.

"House Bill Would End Foreign Policy Curbs on Oil and Gas Equipment to Soviet Union." *U.S. Export Weekly* (June 15, 1982), 412: 404.

Howell, Thomas R. and Alan W. Wolff. "The Role of Trade Law in the Making of Trade Policy." In John H. Jackson, Richard O. Cunningham, Claude G. B. Fontheim, eds., *International Trade Policy: The Lawyer's Perspective*, secs. 3.01–3.06. New York: Matthew Bender, 1985.

Hufbauer, Gary C. and Jeffrey J. Schott. *Economic Sanctions in Support of Foreign Policy Goals.* Washington, D.C.: Institute for International Economics, 1983.

Hufbauer, Gary C. and Jeffrey J. Schott, with Kimberly A. Elliot. *Economic Sanctions Reconsidered: History and Current Policy.* Washington, D.C.: Institute for International Economics, 1985.

Hunt, Cecil. "Multinational Cooperation in Export Controls—The Role of COCOM." *Toledo Law Review* (1983), vol. 14.

Immigration and Nationality Act. 8 U.S.C. sec. 1254 (1976).

Immigration and Naturalization Service v. Chadha. 454 U.S. 812 (1983).

"Immigration and Naturalization Service v. Chadha: The Death Knell for the Legislative Veto." *Iowa Law Review* (1984), 69:512–33.

International Emergency Economic Powers Act. Pub. L. 95-223. 91 Stat. 1626 (1977).

"The International Emergency Economic Powers Act: A Congressional Attempt to Control Presidential Emergency Power." *Harvard Law Review* (March 1983), vol. 96.

International Security Assistance and Arms Export Control Act. Pub. L. 90-629. 82 Stat. 1320 (1968).

"Italy Follows French Stance on Pipeline." *Wall Street Journal*, July 26, 1982, p. 2.

Jackson, John. *World Trade and the Law of GATT.* New York: Bobbs-Merrill, 1969.

Jacobsen, John Kurt and Claus Hofhansel. "Safeguards and Profits Civilian Nuclear Exports, Neo-Marxism, and the Statist Approach." *International Studies Quarterly* (1984), vol. 28.

Jentleson, Bruce W. "From Consensus to Conflict: The Domestic Political Economy of East-West Energy Trade Policy." *International Organization* (Autumn 1984), vol. 38.

BIBLIOGRAPHY 161

Jones, Joseph Marion. *The Fifteen Weeks.* New York: Harcourt, Brace, and World, 1955.
Kegley, Charles W., Jr. and Eugene R. Wittkopf. *American Foreign Policy Pattern and Process*, 3d ed. New York: St. Martin's Press, 1987.
Kissinger, Henry. *The White House Years.* Boston: Little, Brown, 1979.
Klitgaard, Robert E. *National Security and Export Controls.* Santa Monica: RAND Corporation, 1974.
Klutznick, Philip. Secretary of Commerce, Report to Congress Extending Foreign Policy Controls. December 31, 1980. (Mimeo.)
Krasner, Stephen D. "Approaches to the State: Alternative Conceptions and Historical Dynamics." *Comparative Politics* (January 1984), vol. 16.
Krasner, Stephen D. "Are Bureaucracies Important? Allison Wonderland." *Foreign Policy* (Summer 1977), vol. 7.
Krasner, Stephen D. *Defending the National Interest.* Princeton: Princeton University Press, 1978.
Krasner, Stephen D. "United States Commercial and Monetary Policy: Unravelling the Paradox of External Strength and Internal Weakness." In Peter J. Katzenstein, ed., *Between Power and Plenty*, pp. 51–87. Madison: University of Wisconsin Press, 1978.
Lee, L. T. and J. B. McCobb. "United States Trade Embargo of China, 1949–1970: Legal Status and Future Prospects." *New York University Journal of International Law and Policy* (1971), vol. 4.
"Legislation Introduced in House Would Repeal Soviet Foreign Policy Controls." *U.S. Export Weekly* (July 27, 1982), 417:609.
Lowenfeld, A. *International Economic Law: Trade Controls for Political Ends.* 2d ed. New York: Matthew Bender, 1983.
Lowi, Theodore J. "American Business, Public Policy, Case Studies, and Political Theory." *World Politics* (July 1964), 16:667–715.
Lowi, Theodore J. *The End of Liberalism.* New York: Norton, 1969.
McIntyre, John R. "East-West Technology Transfer Policy: Competing Paradigms in Resolving Trade and Strategic Interest Conflicts." *Defense Analysis* (1986), vol. 2.
McIntyre, John R. *Interagency Policy Implementation: The Case of U.S. Export Licensing of Advanced Technology.* Ph.D. dissertation. University of Georgia, 1981.
McIntyre, John R. and Richard T. Cupitt. "East-West Strategic Trade Control: Crumbling Consensus." *Survey* (Spring 1980).
MacKenzie, Kenneth C. *Tariff-Making and Trade Policy in the U.S. and Canada.* New York: Praeger, 1968.
Malloy, Michael P. "Embargo Programs of the United States Treasury Department." *Columbia Journal of Transnational Law* (1981), 20:485–516.
Malmgren, Harold. *Congress and U.S. Trade Policy.* Dallas: LTV Corporation, 1983.

March, James G. and Johan P. Olsen. "The New Institutionalism: Organizational Factors in Political Life." *American Political Science Review* (September 1984), vol. 78.

Marcuss, Stanley J. and Steven D. Mathias. "U.S. Foreign Policy Export Controls: Do They Pass Muster Under International Law?" *International Tax and Business Lawyer* (1984), 2:1–28.

Marcuss, Stanley J. and Eric L. Richard. "Extraterritorial Jurisdiction in United States Trade Law: The Need for A Consistent Theory." *Columbia Journal of Transnational Law* (1981), vol. 20.

Mastanduno, Michael. "The American State and East-West Trade Policy During the Hegemonic Period." Paper presented at American Political Science Association, New Orleans, August 28–September 1, 1985.

"Memorandum of Conversation by the Acting Advisor to the Division of Occupied Areas Economic Affairs," March 16, 1948. *Foreign Relations of the United States: 1948*, vol. 4, *Eastern Europe: The Soviet Union*. Washington, D. C.: GPO, 1974.

"Mexico Joins Critics of U.S. Embargo Against Nicaragua." *Washington Post*, May 5, 1985, p. A21.

Mills, C. W. *The Power Elite*. New York: Oxford University Press, 1956.

Moyer, Homer E. and Linda A. Mabry. "Export Controls as Instruments for Foreign Policy: The History, Legal Issues, and Policy Lessons of Three Recent Cases." *Law and Policy in International Business* (1983), vol. 15.

Mutual Defense Assistance Control Act (Battle Act). Pub. L. 82-213. 65 Stat. 644 (1951).

National Academy of Sciences and National Academy of Engineering. *Briefing: Export Control—Reconciling National Objectives*. Washington, D. C., 1984.

National Emergencies Act. Pub. L. 94-412. 90 Stat. 1255 (1976).

"Note, Accountability, and the Foreign Commerce Power: A Case Study of the Regulation of Exports." *Georgia Journal of International and Comparative Law* (1979), vol. 9.

Odell, John. *U.S. International Monetary Policy*. Princeton: Princeton University Press, 1982.

O'Leary, Michael Kent. *The Politics of American Foreign Aid*. New York: Atherton Press, 1967.

Owens, Henry and Charles L. Schultze, eds. *Setting National Priorities: The Next Ten Years*. Washington, D. C.: Brookings Institution, 1976.

Parrott, Bruce, ed. *Trade, Technology, and Soviet-American Relations*. Bloomington: Indiana University Press, 1985.

Pastor, Robert A. *Congress and the Politics of U.S. Foreign Economic Policy, 1929–1976*. Berkeley: University of California Press, 1980.

Pastor, Robert A. "The Cry and Sigh Syndrome: Congress and Trade

Policy." In A. Schick, ed., *Making Economic Policy in Congress*. Washington, D. C.: American Enterprise Institute, 1983.
Pitkin, Hannah. *The Concept of Representation*. Berkeley: University of California Press, 1976.
"President Orders Halt to Trade With Nicaragua." *Washington Post*, May 2, 1985, pp. A1, A35.
Proposals for Reform of Export Controls for Advanced Technology. Washington, D. C.: American Enterprise Institute, 1979.
The Reciprocal Trade Agreements Act of 1934. 48 Stat. 943 (1934).
Report of the President's Task Force to Improve Administration Licensing Procedures. Washington, D. C., 1976.
Ripley, Randall B. and Grace A. Franklin. *Congress, the Bureaucracy, and Public Policy*. Homewood, Ill.: Dorsey Press, 1980.
Robinson, James A. *Congress and Foreign Policy-Making*. Homewood, Ill.: Dorsey Press, 1962.
Rosenau, James N. *The Scientific Study of Foreign Policy*. New York: Nichols, 1980.
Rosenberg, Mark L. "The World After Chadha: Can Congress Still Control the Agencies?" *Federal Bar News Journal* (September/October 1983), vol. 30.
Rosenblom, David. "Forms of Bureaucratic Representation in the Federal Service." *Midwest Review of Public Administration* (July 1974), vol. 8.
Rosenthal, Douglas and William Knighton. *National Laws and International Commerce: The Problem of Extraterritoriality*. London: Routledge and Kegan Paul, 1982.
Schattschneider, E. E. *Politics, Pressures, and the Tariff*. Englewood Cliffs, N.J.: Prentice Hall, 1935.
Schurmann, Franz. *The Logic of World Power*. New York: Pantheon, 1974.
Skocpol, Theda. "Bringing the State Back In: Current Research." In Peter B. Evans, Dietrich Rueschemeyer, and Theda Skocpol, eds., *Bringing The State Back In*. Cambridge: Cambridge University Press, 1985.
Skol, A. G. and C. H. Peterson. "Export Control Laws and Multinational Enterprise." *International Lawyer* (1977), vol. 11.
Skowronek, Stephen. *Building a New American State: The Expansion of National Administrative Capacities*. New York: Cambridge University Press, 1982.
Sommerfield, S. L. "Treasury Regulations of Foreign Assets and Trade." In W. S. Surry and Donald Wallace, eds., *A Lawyer's Guide to International Business Transactions*. Washington, D. C.: American Bar Association, 1977.
Spero, Joan Edelman. *The Politics of International Economic Relations*. 3d ed. New York: St. Martin's Press, 1985.

Stein, Arthur A. "The Hegemon's Dilemma: Great Britain, the United States, and the International Economic Order." *International Organization* (Spring 1984), vol. 38.

Stern, Paula. *The Water's Edge: Domestic Politics and the Making of American Foreign Policy*. Westport, Conn.: Greenwood Press, 1979.

Stone, Julius. *Legal Controls of International Conflict*. New York: Rinehart, 1954.

Summers, R. S. "Naive Instrumentalism and the Law." P. M. J. Hacker and J. Raz, eds., *Law, Morality, and Society*. Oxford: Clarendon Press, 1977.

Trading with the Enemy Act of 1917. 55 Stat. 839 (1941). As amended 50 U.S.C. app. sec. 1–44 (1982).

Treasury Department Regulations. 31 *Code of Federal Regulations*, pt. 500 *et seq.* 1987.

Truman, David. *The Governmental Process*. New York: Knopf, 1951.

"United States Jurisdiction over Foreign Subsidiaries: Corporate and International Law Aspects." *Law and Policy in International Business* (1983), 15:319–400.

U.S. Bureau of the Census. *Statistical Abstracts of the United States: 1951*. Washington, D. C., 1950.

——*Statistical Abstracts of the United States: 1984*. Washington, D. C., 1983.

U.S. Congress. Comptroller General. *Administration of U.S. Export Licensing Should Be Consolidated to Be More Responsive to Industry*. October 31, 1978.

——*Export Control Regulation Could Be Reduced Without Affecting National Security*. May 26, 1982.

——*Export Controls: Need to Clarify and Simplify Administration*. March 1, 1979.

——*The Government's Role in East-West Trade—Problems and Issues*. February 4, 1976.

U.S. Congress. House. Committee on Banking and Currency. *Export Control Act of 1949 Hearings*. 81st Cong., 1st. sess., 1949.

U.S. Congress. House. Committee on Banking and Currency, Subcommittee on International Trade. *Hearings to Extend and Amend the Export Act of 1949*. 91st Cong., 1st sess., 1969.

U.S. Congress. House. Committee on Banking, Housing, and Urban Affairs. *Reauthorization of the Export Administration Act*. 98th Cong., 1st sess., 1983.

U.S. Congress. House. Committee on Foreign Affairs. *An Assessment of the Afghanistan Sanctions: Implications for Trade and Diplomacy in the 1980s*. 97th Cong., 1st sess., 1981.

——*Export Administration Amendments Act of 1981*. 97th Cong., 1st sess., 1981.

U.S. Congress. House. Committee on Foreign Affairs. *Extension and Revision of the Export Administration Act of 1969.* 96th Cong., 1st sess., 1979.
——*Foreign Policy Export Controls.* 99th Cong., 2d sess., 1986.
——*Iranian Asset Controls.* 96th Congress., 2d sess., 1980.
U.S. Congress. House. Committee on Foreign Affairs, Subcommittee on International Economic Policy and Trade. *Oversight of the Foreign Availability Provisions of the Export Administration Act.* 99th Cong., 2d sess., 1986.
——*Prepared Statement of Lionel H. Olmer, Under Secretary for Trade Administration, Department of Commerce.* 98th Cong., 1st sess., 1983.
U.S. Congress. House. Committee on International Relations. *Export Licensing: Foreign Availability of Stretch Forming Presses.* 95th Cong., 2d sess., 1977.
——*Extension of the Export Administration Act of 1969.* 95th Cong., 1st sess., 1977.
——*Extension and Revision of the Export Administration Act. of 1969.* 95th Cong., 1st sess., 1977.
——*Trading with the Enemy Act Reform Legislation.* H. Rept. 459, 95th Cong., 1st sess., 1977.
U.S. Congress. House. *Export Administration Amendments of 1977.* H. Rept. 190. 95th Cong., 1st sess., 1977.
U.S. Congress. House. *Export Control Act Extension.* H. Rept. 524. 91st Cong., 1st sess., 1969.
U.S. Congress. House. *International Economic Policy Act of 1972.* H. Rept. 1260. 92d Cong., 2d sess., 1972.
U.S. Congress. House. *Investigation and Study of the Administration, Operation, and Enforcement of the Export Control Act of 1949 and Related Acts.* 87th Cong., 1st sess., 1961.
U.S. Congress. House. *Trading with the Enemy Act Reform Legislation.* H. Rept. 459. 95th Cong., 1st sess., 1977.
U.S. Congress. Joint Economic Committee. *Soviet Pipeline Sanctions: The European Perspective.* 97th Cong., 2d sess., 1982.
U.S. Congress. Library of Congress. Congressional Research Service. *Administration of Export Controls.* Washington, D. C.: GPO, 1969.
——*Soviet Pipeline Report.* Washington, D. C.: GPO, 1982.
U.S. Congress. Office of Technology Assessment. *Technology and East-West Trade.* Washington, D. C., 1979.
U.S. Congress. Senate. Committee on Banking and Currency. *Extension of Export Controls.* 81st Cong., 1st sess., 1949.
U.S. Congress. Senate. Committee on Banking and Currency, Subcommittee on International Finance. *Export Expansion and Regulation: Hearings.* 91st Cong., 1st sess., 1969.
U.S. Congress. Senate. Committee on Banking, Housing, and Urban

Affairs. *Equal Export Opportunity Act and the International Economic Policy Act of 1972.* S. Rept. 890. 92d Cong., 2d sess., 1972.

——*Export Control Policy and Extension of the Export Administration Act.* 96th Cong., 1st sess., 1979.

——*Export Expansion and Regulation Act.* S. Rept. 336. 89th Cong., 1st sess., 1969.

——*Extension of the Export Administration Act.* 94th Cong., 2d sess., 1976.

——*Proposed Trans-Siberian Natural Gas Pipeline.* 97th Cong., 1st sess., 1981.

——Reauthorization of the Export Administration Act. 98th Cong., 1st sess., 1983.

U.S. Congress. Senate. Committee on Government Operations, Subcommittee on Investigations. *Settlements of Industry Officials: Hearings.* 84th Cong., 2d sess., 1956.

U.S. Congress. Senate. *The Export Administration Act Amendments of 1983.* S. Rept. to Accompany S. 979. 98th Cong., 1st sess., 1983.

U.S. Congress. Senate. *Export Expansion and Regulation Act.* S. Rept. 336. 91st Cong., 1st sess., 1969.

U.S. Congress. Senate. Memorandum from the Department of Justice for the Special Committee on the Termination of the National Emergency Dated May 21, 1973. 93d Cong., 2d sess., October 7, 1974.

U.S. Congress. Senate. *Senator Jackson Speaking for the Amendment to the Trade Act of 1972.* 92d Cong., 2d sess., 1972. *Congressional Record* 118:33,658.

U.S. Congress. Senate. *Senator Maybank on Reporting Out the Export Control Act of 1949.* 81st Cong., 1st sess., February 7, 1949. *Congressional Record*, p. 949.

U.S. Department of Commerce. "Commodity Control List: Restriction on the Export of Marketable Phosphate Rock, Phosphoric Acid of All Concentrations, and Processed Phosphatic Fertilizers of All Concentrations to the U.S.S.R." 47 *Federal Register* 8293 (February 7, 1980).

U.S. Department of Commerce. "Controls on Exports of Petroleum Equipment to the U.S.S.R., Estonia, Latvia, and Lithuania." 43 *Federal Register* 33,699 (August 1, 1978).

U.S. Department of Commerce. *Export Administration Annual Report for the Fiscal Year 1980.* Washington, D. C.: GPO.

U.S. Department of Commerce. *Export Administration Annual Report for the Fiscal Year 1982.* Washington, D. C.: GPO.

U.S. Department of Commerce. *Export Administration Annual Report for the Year 1983.* Washington, D. C.: GPO.

U.S. Department of Commerce. *Export Administration Annual, Semi-Annual, and Quarterly Reports for the Fiscal Years 1969–1979.* Washington, D.C.: GPO.

U.S. Department of Commerce. *Export Control.* 61st Quarterly Report (1962). Washington, D. C.: GPO.

U.S. Department of Commerce. Order no. 390. 10 *Federal Register* 13,130 (1945).

U.S. Department of Commerce. Remarks of President Johnson at Doylestown, Penn., October 16, 1966. *Weekly Compilation of Presidential Documents* vol. 2, 31 *Federal Register* 13,699 (1966).

U.S. Department of Commerce. "Restriction on Exports for the Kama River Truck Complex (Kam Az) in the U.S.S.R. of Truck Engine Assembly Lines." 45 *Federal Register* 30,617 (May 9, 1980).

U.S. Department of Commerce. "Restriction on Exports to the Republic of South Africa and Namibia." 43 *Federal Register* 7311 (February 22, 1978).

U.S. Department of Commerce. "Restriction on the Export of Agricultural Commodities and Products to the U.S.S.R." 45 *Federal Register* 1883 (January 9, 1980).

U.S. Department of Commerce. "Revision of Commodity Control List." 43 *Federal Register* 20,484 (May 12, 1978).

U.S. Department of Commerce. "Revision of Commodity Control List." 43 *Federal Register* 43,450 (September 26, 1978).

U.S. Department of Commerce. "Revision of Export Administration Regulations in Support of Human Rights." 43 *Federal Register* 27,985 (June 28, 1978).

U.S. Department of Commerce. "Revision of Policy on Export to Afghanistan." 45 *Federal Register* 37,415 (June 3, 1980).

U.S. Department of Commerce. "Revisions to Reflect Identification and Continuation of Foreign Policy Export Controls." 45 *Federal Register* 1595 (January 8, 1980).

U.S. Department of State. *The Battle Act in New Times: Fifteenth Report to Congress.* 1961.

U.S. General Accounting Office. *Administration Knowledge of Economic Costs of Foreign Policy Controls.* September 2, 1983.

U.S. General Accounting Office. *Export Controls: Assessment of Commerce Department's Foreign Policy Report to Congress.* August 1986.

U.S. National Security Council. "Control of Exports to the U.S.S.R. and Eastern Europe." December 17, 1947. *Foreign Relations of the United States, 1948:* vol. 4, *Eastern Europe; The Soviet Union.* Washington, D. C.: GPO, 1972.

"U.S. Policy Toward European Gas Pipeline." *Gallup Report,* August 1982, p. 13.

U.S. President. Executive Order 12532. "Prohibiting Trade and Certain Other Transactions Involving South Africa." 50 *Federal Register* 36,861 (September 10, 1985).

U.S. President. *Public Papers of the Presidents of the United States: Harry S. Truman, 1947.* Washington, D. C.: Office of the Federal Register, National Archives and Record Service.

U.S. President. Special Report, "Multilateral Export Controls," printed in U.S. Congress. House Committee on International Relations. *Export Administration Act: Agenda for Reform.* 95th Cong., 2d sess., 1977.

U.S. President. "United States Export Policy." *Weekly Compilation of Presidential Documents,* vol. 14, no. 39. September 26, 1978.

U.S. v. Guy W. Capps, Inc. 204 F.2d 655 (4th Cir. 1953).

Verba, Sidney. "Sequences and Development." In Leonard Binder et al., *Crises and Sequences in Political Development.* Princeton: Princeton University Press, 1971.

War Powers Resolution. Pub. L. 93-158. 87 Stat. 555 (1973).

Wilson, Woodrow. "The Study of Administration." In Karl DeSchweinitz, Jr. and Kenneth W. Thompson, eds., *Man and Modern Society.* New York: Henry Holt, 1953.

INDEX

Abbott, Kenneth W., 131n66
Adler-Karlsson, Gunnar, 122n43
Advisory Committee on Export Policy, 122n38, 129n53; *see also* Export licensing
Allison, Graham T., 44, 105, 110n4, 114n30, 116n34, 128n43, 156nn4,6
Ashly, Thomas L., 31

Baize, John, 154n15
Baker, Howard, 144n52
Baldrige, Malcolm, 81, 84, 98, 152n87
Baldwin, David A., 20, 62, 109n3, 110n5, 121n37, 136n28
Baldwin, Robert, 111n15, 156n7
Ball, George, 141n21
Ballagh, Thomas, 23
Barnes, Michael D., 155n15
Battle Act, 18
Bauer, Raymond, 111n10, 114n29
Bennett, Wallace F., 125n13
Berman, Harold J., 119n20, 120n29, 123n51, 127nn37,39, 132n76
Bertsch, Gary, 3, 50, 111n7, 119n17, 131n68
Bingham, Jonathan B., 77, 146n59
Blaisdell, Thomas, 120n29
Block, John, 145n54
Blumenthal, Michael, 132n1
Bonker, Don, 81, 91, 93, 95, 98, 155n15
Brown, Gary, 17
Bureaucratic institutions: autonomy, 8, 43, 46, 53, 66-67, 103-5, 115n31; and continuity in U.S. export control policy, 7, 43-46, 53, 64-65, 104-5, 129n51; and democracy, 7, 115n31; implementation, 48; and instrumentalism, 8; mandates, 9, 19-20, 43, 103-4, 115n32; responsiveness to Congress and exporters, 46-47, 53, 103-4, 128n49, 129n51, 130n60
Bureaucratic politics model, 8-10, 14
Bush, George, 153n87

Carroll, Holbert N., 112n17, 122n42
Carter administration, views on East-West trade policy, 55
Chambers, John A., 64, 65
Chapman, Erskine C., 153n2
Christiansen, Thomas A., 31, 140n19
COCOM: allied cooperation, 17-18, 31, 50-52, 131nn69,70; defined, 17, 49
Cohen, Benjamin, J., 4, 111n11, 156n2
Commodity Control List, 45, 128n46
Congress: and executive, interest group conflict, 36, 45-46; and executive, interest group harmony, 21-24, 27-30; and U.S. export control policy, 11; *see also* Executive
Constitution: shared authority of President and Congress in foreign policy, 6: shared authority of President and Congress in foreign commercial policy, 6, 113n21, 113n22
Cooper, Richard, 139n9

Cranston, Alan, 155*n*15
Cupitt, Richard T., 119*n*16, 130*n*66

Dahl, Robert, 5, 112*n*18
Dajani, M. S., 140*n*20
Daoudi, M. S., 140*n*20
Davis, Kenneth N., 37
Dexter, Lewis, 111*n*10, 114*n*29
Downey, Arthur T., 136*n*26

Economic coercion, *see* Sanctions
Economic Defense Advisory Committee, 51, 131*n*71
Elliott, Kimberly A., 110*n*3
Emergency economic powers, *see* Foreign policy export controls
Equal Export Opportunity Act of 1972, 46
Executive: autonomy, 2, 5, 7, 10, 13, 40-41, 52, 65, 69, 70-71, 75, 77, 83-84, 86-89, 94, 96-99, 101-3, 106, 126*n*24, 127*n*37, 132*n*76; and Congress in U.S. export control policy, 6, 40-41, 52, 65, 76-77, 97, 99, 101-2, 110*n*4, 112*n*16, 156*n*1; and Congress in U.S. foreign policy, 5, 101; and Congress in U.S. trade policy, 111*n*10, 113*nn*21,25
Export Administration Act of 1969: congressional motivations for statutory reform, 30-32; export license processing, 34; foreign availability, 34, 38, 126*n*31; generally, 29; harmonization of U.S. controls with COCOM, 35, 38-39, 130*n*66; House and Senate bills, 33; implementation, 44-52, 128*n*49, 129*n*51, 130*n*62, 131*n*68; legislative outcome, 39-41; minority viewpoint in Congress, 33, 125*n*13; national security controls, 34, 38; Nixon administration opposition to reform, 33-39, 127*n*39 (*see also* Nixon administration); purposes, 29, 33, 125*n*14
Export Administration Act of 1979, *see* Foreign Policy Export Controls
Export Administration Act of 1985: administration position on legislation, 92; bureaucratic implementation of, 96, 99; business community's position on legislation, 92; contract sanctity provision, 94; extraterritoriality, 95, 153*n*8; foreign policy export control provisions, 94-95; House bill, 91; judicial review of agency actions, 95; legislation process generally, 91, 153*n*3; national security controls provisions, 95-96; Senate bill, 91; statutory provisions generally, 93-94
Export Administration Review Board, 122*n*38, 129*n*53; *see also* Export licensing
Export Control Act of 1949: amendments of 1962, 25-26; generally, 15; statutory purposes, 16-17
Export licensing: case review, 20, 62, 66, 129*n*53; generally, 1, 2, 30, 34, 136*n*29, 140*n*16; impact on business of delays, 58-59, 133*nn*7,8, 134*n*11; institutional opposition to reform, 59-60, 64, 66, 137*n*34; interagency review, 20-21, 61-62, 64, 129*n*53, 136*n*27; Operating Committee, 21, 121*n*38; persistence of delay, 21, 61-64, 66, 130*n*62, 134*nn*11,12, 135*n*20, 137*n*37; responsive to Congress and exporters, 140*n*16; role of Department of Commerce, 19-20, 57, 63-64, 136*n*26; role of Department of Defense, 19, 62-64, 135; role of Department of State, 62-64, 135*n*23, 136*n*25; statutory reforms, 56-60, 66, 133*n*5, 134*n*14

Fascell, Dante B., 155*n*16
Fasick, Kenneth J., 59, 63, 139*n*14
Findley, Paul, III, 81, 150*n*68
Fontaine, Andre, 149*n*67
Foreign policy export controls: congressional opposition in the 1980s, 79-83, 98, 144*n*52, 145*nn*53,56, 149*n*68, 154*n*15, 155*n*16; consultation requirements, 76, 83-88, 139*n*14, 143*n*42, 152*n*86, 155*n*16; cooperation with allies, 72; economic costs of, 85-86, 148*n*67; executive opposition to statutory

reforms of 1979, 74, 141n26, 142nn27,28,29; extraterritorial extension of, 80-82, 145n59, 146nn61,62, 147n63, 148nn65,66,67, 149n68; following Soviet invasion of Afghanistan, 78-80, 89; foreign availability assessment, 71-75, 84, 141nn23,25,26; generally, 69-71, 88, 89; impact on reputation of U.S. exporters, 72; International Emergency Economic Powers Act (IEEPA) as a statutory vehicle for, 83, 97, 144n50, 154n15, 155n16; international opposition in the 1980s, 81-83, 98, 146n62, 147n63, 148n67, 154n15; Reagan administration use of, 80-82, 89; required findings, 73-74, 76, 78, 84, 86, 139n14, 141n23, 150n74, 151n77, 152n85; statutory reforms of the Export Administration Act of 1979, 71-77; use prior to 1979, 69-71, 138nn2,3-7, 130n9
Freed, Louis, I., 24
Freedenberg, Paul, 154n9

Garn, Jake, 84
Garson, John R., 119n20, 120n29, 123n51, 132n76
Garthoff, Raymond, 126n24
Genscher, Hans-Dietrich, 154n15
Ginzburg, Aleksandr, 56, 139n9
Glitman, Maynard W., 136n25
Goldstein, Judith, 121n34
Grain boycott of Soviet Union, 78-80, 89
Gray, James A., 58, 134n11, 141n24
Greenwald, Joseph A., 36

Haig, Alexander, Jr., 81, 145n54, 146n61
Hall, Michael, 154n15
Halperin, Morton T., 115n30, 156n6
Harriman, Averell, 119n17
Heinz, John, 84, 87, 91, 93
Henkin, Louis, 113n21
Howell, Thomas R., 116n38
Hufbauer, Gary C., 109n3, 141n20
Huszagh, Fredrick W., 64, 137n33

Institutions, *see* Bureaucratic Institutions

Jackson, Henry, 42, 127n40
Jackson-Vanik Amendment, 42, 55
Jentleson, Bruce W., 22, 26, 122n40, 123n61
Jepsen, Roger, 149n67
Johnson administration, views on East-West trade policy, 27
Jones, Joseph Marion, 119n15

Kama River, 79
Kanter, Arnold, 156n6
Karth, Joseph E., 134n8
Kennedy administration, views on East-West trade policy, 25-27
Kissinger, Henry, 35, 36, 42, 126nn20,24, 128n48
Kitchen, Paul, 25
Klitgaard, Robert A., 131n68
Klutznick, Philip, 150n73
Krasner, Stephen D., 30, 110n4, 111n10, 114n26, 116n35, 124n2

Lesher, Richard L., 81
Liberalism, and U.S. foreign policy, 114n26
Licensing, *see* Export licensing
Lindstrom, Talbot, 96
Lowi, Theodore, 65, 111n6, 115n33

Mabry, Linda A., 150n68
McIntyre, John R., 119n16, 120nn28,32, 130n66
MacKenzie, Kenneth C., 113n23
McLellan, Robert, 140n19, 141n25
Malmgren, Harold, 111n14
March, James G., 114n27
Marcuss, Stanley, 142n28, 143n37
Marxism, 114n26
Mastanduno, Michael, 26, 27, 43, 116n2, 123n59, 124nn62,64, 128n42
Methodology, 11
Michel, Robert, 81, 154n15
Miles, Clarence R., 23
Mondale, Walter, 31, 124n5
Motley, Langhorne A., 155n16
Moyer, Homer E., 150n68
Multilateral Coordinating Committee on Export Controls, *see* COCOM
Muskie, Edmund, 124nn4,7

INDEX

Mutual Defense Assistance Control Act, 18
Mutual Security Act, 18, 24

Nixon administration, views on East-West trade policy, 30, 33-39, 41, 43, 103, 127n39, 128n48
Nutter, G. Warren, 37, 39

O'Day, Paul T., 61
Office of Export Controls, see Origins of U.S. export controls
Office of International Trade, see Origins of U.S. export controls
Olmer, Lionel, 61, 92, 135n22
Olsen, Johan P., 114n27
Olympic boycott, 78-79
Operating Committee, see Export licensing
Organizational politics model, 105, 106
Origins of U.S. export control policy: congressional-executive-interest group harmony, 14-15; institutions, 18-19, 120nn28,29, 121nn36,49, 123n56 (see also Export licensing); role of ideology, 13, 118n10-11, 119n17, 120n32, 121n34 (see also Export Control Act of 1949); structural factors, 14; and U.S. hegemony, 14, 119n18

Packard, David, 141n21
Parrott, Bruce, 111n7
Pastor, Robert A., 4, 111n13, 112n16, 113n25, 116n36
Percy, Charles, 81
Perle, Richard, 92
Pipeline controls, 81-83, 87
Pitkin, Hannah, 115n31
Pluralism: and U.S. export control policy, 3-4, 23, 101; and U.S. trade policy, 4, 110nn5,6, 114n29
Pool, Ithiel de Sola, 111n10, 114n29
Proxmire, William, 142n27
Public choice theory, 106

Robinson, James A., 112n17, 113n20
Root, William A., 138n2

Rosenau, James N., 104, 105, 156n3
Rosenblom, David, 115n31
Rusk, Dean, 120n31
Rusk Center, 63, 64, 137n33

Sanctions, 1, 2, 109n3, 140n20
Scharansky, Anatoly, 56, 139
Schattschneider, E. E., 111n10
Schneider, William Jr., 153n8
Schott, Jeffrey J., 110n3, 141n20
Schurmann, Franz, 115n32
Shields, Roger E., 135n24
Sinclair, Joseph A., 23, 122n49
Skocpol, Theda, 114nn26,28,30, 116n39
South African sanctions, 98-99, 155n18, 156n20
Spence, Eldon, 22
Spero, Joan Edelman, 132n1
Stans, Maurice, 33
Statism and U.S. foreign policy, 114nn26,28, 116n2
Stein, Arthur A., 119n18
Stern, Paula, 127n41
Stevenson, Adlai, 144n52
Stewart, Charles W., 146n59
Strauss, Robert, 112n16
Sundquist, James L., 41, 127n38
Swingle, William S., 23
Szanton, Peter, 110n4, 116n34

TASS, 56, 142n27, 139n9
Technical Advisory Committees, 47-48
Tower, John G., 125n13
Trade Advisory Committees, 96, 130n60
Trading with the Enemy Act, 117n3

U.S.-Soviet trade agreements of 1972, see Jackson-Vanik Amendment

Widall, William B., 33
Williams, Harrison, 32
Wilson, Woodrow, 115n31
Wolff, Alan W., 116n38

Zablocki, Clement, 143n43